DONATED BY AA MEMBERS
DISTRIBUTED BY THE HOSPITAL
AND INSTITUTION COMMITTEE
OF NORTHERN CALIFORNIA

D0466161

TWELVE STEPS
and
TWELVE TRADITIONS

TWELVE
STEPS
and
TWELVE
TRADITIONS

ALCOHOLICS ANONYMOUS® WORLD SERVICES, INC.
BOX 459, GRAND CENTRAL STATION
NEW YORK, NY 10163

Copyright © 1952, 1953, 1981 by AA Grapevine, Inc.
and Alcoholics Anonymous Publishing
(now known as Alcoholics Anonymous World Services, Inc.)

All rights reserved.
First Printing, April 1953
First Printing of Gift Edition, 1965
Forty-fourth Printing, 2018

*This is A.A. General Service
Conference-approved literature.*

Mail address:
Box 459, Grand Central Station
New York, NY 10163

www.aa.org

Alcoholics Anonymous® and A.A.® are registered trademarks
of Alcoholics Anonymous World Services, Inc.

ISBN 978-0-916856-06-9

Library of Congress Catalog Card No. 53-5454

Printed in the United States of America

5M – 11/18 (CM)   B-4

Contents

"We admitted we were powerless over alcohol—that our lives had become unmanageable."

Who cares to admit complete defeat? Admission of powerlessness is the first step in liberation. Relation of humility to sobriety. Mental obsession plus physical allergy. Why must every A.A. hit bottom?

"Came to believe that a Power greater than ourselves could restore us to sanity."

What can we believe in? A.A. does not demand belief; Twelve Steps are only suggestions. Importance of an open mind. Variety of ways to faith. Substitution of A.A. as Higher Power. Plight of the disillusioned. Roadblocks of indifference and prejudice. Lost faith found in A.A. Problems of intellectuality and self-sufficiency. Negative and positive thinking. Self-righteousness. Defiance is an outstanding characteristic of alcoholics. Step Two is a rallying point to sanity. Right relation to God.

"Made a decision to turn our will and our lives over to the care of God <u>as we understood Him</u>."

Step Three is like opening of a locked door. How shall we let God into our lives? Willingness is the key. Dependence as a means to independence. Dangers of self-sufficiency. Turning our will over to Higher Power. Misuse of willpower. Sustained and personal exertion necessary to conform to God's will.

for objective—and perfection. Why we must keep trying. "Being ready" is all-important. Necessity of taking action. Delay is dangerous. Rebellion may be fatal. Point at which we abandon limited objectives and move toward God's will for us.

Step Seven   70

What is humility? What can it mean to us? The avenue to true freedom of the human spirit. Necessary aid to survival. Value of ego-puncturing. Failure and misery transformed by humility. Strength from weakness. Pain is the admission price to new life. Self-centered fear chief activator of defects. Step Seven is change in attitude which permits us to move out of ourselves toward God.

Step Eight   77

This and the next two Steps are concerned with personal relations. Learning to live with others is a fascinating adventure. Obstacles: reluctance to forgive; nonadmission of wrongs to others; purposeful forgetting. Necessity of exhaustive survey of past. Deepening insight results from thoroughness. Kinds of harm done to others. Avoiding extreme judgments. Taking the objective view. Step Eight is the beginning of the end of isolation.

Step Nine   83

A tranquil mind is the first requisite for good judgment. Good timing is important in making amends. What is courage? Prudence means taking calculated chances. Amends begin when we join A.A. Peace of mind cannot be bought at the expense of others. Need for discretion. Readiness to take consequences of our past and to take responsibility for well-being of others is spirit of Step Nine.

Step Ten   88

"Continued to take personal inventory and when we were wrong promptly admitted it."

Can we stay sober and keep emotional balance under all conditions? Self-searching becomes a regular habit. Admit, accept, and patiently correct defects. Emotional hangover. When past is settled with, present challenges can be met. Varieties of inventory. Anger, resentments, jealousy, envy, self-pity, hurt pride—all led to the bottle. Self-restraint first objective. Insurance against "big-shot-ism." Let's look at credits as well as debits. Examination of motives.

Step Eleven   96

"Sought through prayer and meditation to improve our conscious contact with God <u>*as we understood Him*</u>, *praying only for knowledge of His will for us and the power to carry that out."*

Meditation and prayer main channels to Higher Power. Connection between self-examination and meditation and prayer. An unshakable foundation for life. How shall we meditate? Meditation has no boundaries. An individual adventure. First result is emotional balance. What about prayer? Daily petitions for understanding of God's will and grace to carry it out. Actual results of prayer are beyond question. Rewards of meditation and prayer.

Step Twelve   106

"Having had a spiritual awakening as the result of these steps, we tried to carry this message to alcoholics, and to practice these principles in all our affairs."

Joy of living is the theme of the Twelfth Step. Action its keyword. Giving that asks no reward. Love that has no price tag. What is spiritual awakening? A new state of consciousness and being is received as a free gift. Readiness to receive gift lies in practice of Twelve Steps. The magnificent reality. Rewards of helping other alcoholics. Kinds of Twelfth Step work. Problems of Twelfth Step work. What about the practice of these principles in *all* our affairs? Monotony, pain, and calamity turned to good use by practice of Steps. Difficulties of practice. "Two-stepping." Switch to "twelve-stepping" and demonstrations of faith. Growing spiritually is the answer to our problems. Placing spiritual growth first. Domination and overdependence. Putting our lives on give-and-take basis. Dependence upon God necessary to recovery of alcoholics. "Practicing these principles in *all* our affairs": Domestic relations in A.A. Outlook upon material matters changes. So do feelings about personal importance. Instincts restored to true purpose. Understanding is key to right attitudes, right action key to good living.

THE TWELVE TRADITIONS

our group conscience. Our leaders are but trusted servants; they do not govern."

Where does A.A. get its direction? Sole authority in A.A. is loving God as He may express Himself in the group conscience. Formation of a group. Growing pains. Rotating committees are servants of the group. Leaders do not govern, they serve. Does A.A. have a real leadership? "Elder statesmen" and "bleeding deacons." The group conscience speaks.

Better do one thing well than many badly. The life of our Fellowship depends on this principle. The ability of each A.A. to identify himself with and bring recovery to the newcomer is a gift from God... passing on this gift to others is our one aim. Sobriety can't be kept unless it is given away.

Tradition Six

"An A.A. group ought never endorse, finance, or lend the A.A. name to any related facility or outside enterprise, lest problems of money, property, and prestige divert us from our primary purpose."

Experience proved that we could not endorse any related enterprise, no matter how good. We could not be all things to all men. We saw that we could not lend the A.A. name to any outside activity.

Tradition Seven

"Every A.A. group ought to be fully self-supporting, declining outside contributions."

No A.A. Tradition had the labor pains this one did. Collective poverty initially a matter of necessity. Fear of exploitation. Necessity of separating the spiritual from the material. Decision to subsist on A.A. voluntary contributions only. Placing the responsibility of supporting A.A. headquarters directly upon A.A. members. Bare running expenses plus a prudent reserve is headquarters policy.

Tradition Eight

"Alcoholics Anonymous should remain forever non-professional, but our service centers may employ special workers."

You can't mix the Twelfth Step and money. Line of cleavage between voluntary Twelfth Step work and paid-for services. A.A. could not function without full-time service workers. Professional workers are not professional A.A.'s. Relation of A.A. to industry, education, etc. Twelfth Step work is never paid for, but those who labor in service for us are worthy of their hire.

Tradition Nine   172

> *"A.A., as such, ought never be organized; but we may
> create service boards or committees directly responsible
> to those they serve."*

Special service boards and committees. The General
Service Conference, the board of trustees, and group
committees cannot issue directives to A.A. members
or groups. A.A.'s can't be dictated to—individually or
collectively. Absence of coercion works because unless
each A.A. follows suggested Steps to recovery, he signs
his own death warrant. Same condition applies to the
group. Suffering and love are A.A.'s disciplinarians. Difference between spirit of authority and spirit of service.
Aim of our services is to bring sobriety within reach of
all who want it.

Tradition Ten   176

> *"Alcoholics Anonymous has no opinion on outside is-
> sues; hence the A.A. name ought never be drawn into
> public controversy."*

A.A. does not take sides in any public controversy. Reluctance to fight is not a special virtue. Survival and spread of
A.A. are our primary aims. Lessons learned from Washingtonian movement.

Tradition Eleven   180

> *"Our public relations policy is based on attraction rath-
> er than promotion; we need always maintain personal
> anonymity at the level of press, radio, and films."*

Public relations are important to A.A. Good public relations save lives. We seek publicity for A.A. principles,
not A.A. members. The press has cooperated. Personal
anonymity at the public level is the cornerstone of our
public relations policy. Eleventh Tradition is a constant reminder that personal ambition has no place in
A.A. Each member becomes an active guardian of our
Fellowship.

Tradition Twelve

"Anonymity is the spiritual foundation of all our traditions, ever reminding us to place principles before personalities."

Spiritual substance of anonymity is sacrifice. Subordinating personal aims to the common good is the essence of all Twelve Traditions. Why A.A. could not remain a secret society. Principles come before personalities. One hundred percent anonymity at the public level. Anonymity is real humility.

The Twelve Traditions—the Long Form

Introduction

ALCOHOLICS ANONYMOUS first published *Twelve Steps and Twelve Traditions* in 1953. Bill W., who along with Dr. Bob S. founded Alcoholics Anonymous in 1935, wrote the book to share 18 years of collective experience within the Fellowship on how A.A. members recover, and how our society functions.

In recent years some members and friends of A.A. have asked if it would be wise to update the language, idioms, and historical references in the book to present a more contemporary image for the Fellowship. However, because the book has helped so many alcoholics find recovery, there exists strong sentiment within the Fellowship against any change to it. In fact, the 2002 General Service Conference discussed this issue and it was unanimously recommended that: "The text in the book *Twelve Steps and Twelve Traditions*, written by Bill W., remain as is, recognizing the Fellowship's feelings that Bill's writing be retained as originally published."

We hope that the collective spiritual experience of the A.A. pioneers captured in these pages continues to help alcoholics and friends of A.A. understand the principles of our program.

Foreword

ALCOHOLICS ANONYMOUS is a worldwide fellowship of more than one hundred thousand* alcoholic men and women who are banded together to solve their common problems and to help fellow sufferers in recovery from that age-old, baffling malady, alcoholism.

This book deals with the "Twelve Steps" and the "Twelve Traditions" of Alcoholics Anonymous. It presents an explicit view of the principles by which A.A. members recover and by which their Society functions.

A.A.'s Twelve Steps are a group of principles, spiritual in their nature, which, if practiced as a way of life, can expel the obsession to drink and enable the sufferer to become happily and usefully whole.

A.A.'s Twelve Traditions apply to the life of the Fellowship itself. They outline the means by which A.A. maintains its unity and relates itself to the world about it, the way it lives and grows.

Though the essays which follow were written mainly for members, it is thought by many of A.A.'s friends that these pieces might arouse interest and find application outside A.A. itself.

Many people, nonalcoholics, report that as a result of the practice of A.A.'s Twelve Steps, they have been able to

---

* In 2018, it is estimated that over two million have recovered through A.A.

meet other difficulties of life. They think that the Twelve
Steps can mean more than sobriety for problem drinkers.
They see in them a way to happy and effective living for
many, alcoholic or not.

There is, too, a rising interest in the Twelve Traditions
of Alcoholics Anonymous. Students of human relations
are beginning to wonder how and why A.A. functions as a
society. Why is it, they ask, that in A.A. no member can be
set in personal authority over another, that nothing like a
central government can anywhere be seen? How can a set
of traditional principles, having no legal force at all, hold
the Fellowship of Alcoholics Anonymous in unity and effectiveness? The second section of this volume, though designed for A.A.'s membership, will give such inquirers an
inside view of A.A. never before possible.

Alcoholics Anonymous began in 1935 at Akron, Ohio,
as the outcome of a meeting between a well-known sur-
geon and a New York broker. Both were severe cases of
alcoholism and were destined to become co-founders of
the A.A. Fellowship.

The basic principles of A.A., as they are known today,
were borrowed mainly from the fields of religion and medicine, though some ideas upon which success finally depended were the result of noting the behavior and needs of
the Fellowship itself.

After three years of trial and error in selecting the most
workable tenets upon which the Society could be based,
and after a large amount of failure in getting alcoholics to
recover, three successful groups emerged—the first at Akron, the second at New York, and the third at Cleveland.

Even then it was hard to find twoscore of sure recoveries in all three groups.

Nevertheless, the infant Society determined to set down its experience in a book which finally reached the public in April 1939. At this time the recoveries numbered about one hundred. The book was called "Alcoholics Anonymous," and from it the Fellowship took its name. In it alcoholism was described from the alcoholic's point of view, the spiritual ideas of the Society were codified for the first time in the Twelve Steps, and the application of these Steps to the alcoholic's dilemma was made clear. The remainder of the book was devoted to thirty stories or case histories in which the alcoholics described their drinking experiences and recoveries. This established identification with alcoholic readers and proved to them that the virtually impossible had now become possible. The book "Alcoholics Anonymous" became the basic text of the Fellowship, and it still is. This present volume proposes to broaden and deepen the understanding of the Twelve Steps as first written in the earlier work.

With the publication of the book "Alcoholics Anonymous" in 1939, the pioneering period ended and a prodigious chain reaction set in as the recovered alcoholics carried their message to still others. In the next years alcoholics flocked to A.A. by tens of thousands, largely as the result of excellent and continuous publicity freely given by magazines and newspapers throughout the world. Clergymen and doctors alike rallied to the new movement, giving it unstinted support and endorsement.

This startling expansion brought with it very severe

growing pains. Proof that alcoholics could recover had been made. But it was by no means sure that such great numbers of yet erratic people could live and work together with harmony and good effect.

Everywhere there arose threatening questions of membership, money, personal relations, public relations, management of groups, clubs, and scores of other perplexities. It was out of this vast welter of explosive experience that A.A.'s Twelve Traditions took form and were first published in 1946 and later confirmed at A.A.'s First International Convention, held at Cleveland in 1950. The Tradition section of this volume portrays in some detail the experience which finally produced the Twelve Traditions and so gave A.A. its present form, substance, and unity.

As A.A. now enters maturity, it has begun to reach into forty foreign lands.[*] In the view of its friends, this is but the beginning of its unique and valuable service.

It is hoped that this volume will afford all who read it a close-up view of the principles and forces which have made Alcoholics Anonymous what it is.

(A.A.'s General Service Office may be reached by writing:
Alcoholics Anonymous, P.O. Box 459,
Grand Central Station, New York, NY 10163. U.S.A.)

---

[*] In 2018, A.A. is established in approximately 180 countries.

THE TWELVE STEPS

Step One

*"We admitted we were powerless over alcohol—
that our lives had become unmanageable."*

WHO cares to admit complete defeat? Practically no one,
of course. Every natural instinct cries out against the idea
of personal powerlessness. It is truly awful to admit that,
glass in hand, we have warped our minds into such an obsession for destructive drinking that only an act of Providence can remove it from us.

No other kind of bankruptcy is like this one. Alcohol,
now become the rapacious creditor, bleeds us of all self-
sufficiency and all will to resist its demands. Once this stark
fact is accepted, our bankruptcy as going human concerns
is complete.

But upon entering A.A. we soon take quite another view
of this absolute humiliation. We perceive that only through
utter defeat are we able to take our first steps toward liberation and strength. Our admissions of personal powerlessness finally turn out to be firm bedrock upon which happy
and purposeful lives may be built.

We know that little good can come to any alcoholic
who joins A.A. unless he has first accepted his devastating weakness and all its consequences. Until he so humbles
himself, his sobriety—if any—will be precarious. Of real
happiness he will find none at all. Proved beyond doubt by
an immense experience, this is one of the facts of A.A. life.

The principle that we shall find no enduring strength until we first admit complete defeat is the main taproot from which our whole Society has sprung and flowered.

When first challenged to admit defeat, most of us revolted. We had approached A.A. expecting to be taught self-confidence. Then we had been told that so far as alcohol is concerned, self-confidence was no good whatever; in fact, it was a total liability. Our sponsors declared that we were the victims of a mental obsession so subtly powerful that no amount of human willpower could break it. There was, they said, no such thing as the personal conquest of this compulsion by the unaided will. Relentlessly deepening our dilemma, our sponsors pointed out our increasing sensitivity to alcohol—an allergy, they called it. The tyrant alcohol wielded a double-edged sword over us: first we were smitten by an insane urge that condemned us to go on drinking, and then by an allergy of the body that insured we would ultimately destroy ourselves in the process. Few indeed were those who, so assailed, had ever won through in singlehanded combat. It was a statistical fact that alcoholics almost never recovered on their own resources. And this had been true, apparently, ever since man had first crushed grapes.

In A.A.'s pioneering time, none but the most desperate cases could swallow and digest this unpalatable truth. Even these "last-gaspers" often had difficulty in realizing how hopeless they actually were. But a few did, and when these laid hold of A.A. principles with all the fervor with which the drowning seize life preservers, they almost invariably got well. That is why the first edition of the book "Alcoholics Anonymous," published when our membership was small, dealt with low-bottom cases only. Many less desperate alcoholics tried A.A., but did not succeed because they could not make the admission of hopelessness.

It is a tremendous satisfaction to record that in the following years this changed. Alcoholics who still had their health, their families, their jobs, and even two cars in the garage, began to recognize their alcoholism. As this trend grew, they were joined by young people who were scarcely more than potential alcoholics. They were spared that last ten or fifteen years of literal hell the rest of us had gone through. Since Step One requires an admission that our lives have become unmanageable, how could people such as these take this Step?

It was obviously necessary to raise the bottom the rest of us had hit to the point where it would hit them. By going back in our own drinking histories, we could show that years before we realized it we were out of control, that our drinking even then was no mere habit, that it was indeed the beginning of a fatal progression. To the doubters we could say, "Perhaps you're not an alcoholic after all. Why don't you try some more controlled drinking, bearing in mind meanwhile what we have told you about alcoholism?" This attitude brought immediate and practical results. It was then discovered that when one alcoholic had planted in the mind of another the true nature of his malady, that person could never be the same again. Following every spree, he would say to himself, "Maybe those A.A.'s were right...." After a few such experiences, often years before the onset of extreme difficulties, he would return to us convinced. He had hit bottom as truly as any of us. John Barleycorn himself had become our best advocate.

Why all this insistence that every A.A. must hit bottom first? The answer is that few people will sincerely try to practice the A.A. program unless they have hit bottom. For practicing A.A.'s remaining eleven Steps means the adoption of attitudes and actions that almost no alcoholic who is still drinking can dream of taking. Who wishes to be rigorously honest and tolerant? Who wants to confess his faults to another and make restitution for harm done? Who cares anything about a Higher Power, let alone meditation and prayer? Who wants to sacrifice time and energy in trying to carry A.A.'s message to the next sufferer? No, the average alcoholic, self-centered in the extreme, doesn't care for this prospect—unless he has to do these things in order to stay alive himself.

Under the lash of alcoholism, we are driven to A.A., and there we discover the fatal nature of our situation. Then, and only then, do we become as open-minded to conviction and as willing to listen as the dying can be. We stand ready to do anything which will lift the merciless obsession from us.

Step Two

"Came to believe that a Power greater than ourselves could restore us to sanity."

THE moment they read Step Two, most A.A. newcomers are confronted with a dilemma, sometimes a serious one. How often have we heard them cry out, "Look what you people have done to us! You have convinced us that we are alcoholics and that our lives are unmanageable. Having reduced us to a state of absolute helplessness, you now declare that none but a Higher Power can remove our obsession. Some of us *won't* believe in God, others can't, and still others who do believe that God exists have no faith whatever He will perform this miracle. Yes, you've got us over the barrel, all right—but where do we go from here?"

Let's look first at the case of the one who says he won't believe—the belligerent one. He is in a state of mind which can be described only as savage. His whole philosophy of life, in which he so gloried, is threatened. It's bad enough, he thinks, to admit alcohol has him down for keeps. But now, still smarting from that admission, he is faced with something really impossible. How he does cherish the thought that man, risen so majestically from a single cell in the primordial ooze, is the spearhead of evolution and therefore the only god that his universe knows! Must he renounce all this to save himself?

At this juncture, his A.A. sponsor usually laughs. This, the newcomer thinks, is just about the last straw. This is the beginning of the end. And so it is: the beginning of the end of his old life, and the beginning of his emergence into a new one. His sponsor probably says, "Take it easy. The hoop you have to jump through is a lot wider than you think. At least I've found it so. So did a friend of mine who was a one-time vice-president of the American Atheist Society, but he got through with room to spare."

"Well," says the newcomer, "I know you're telling me the truth. It's no doubt a fact that A.A. is full of people who once believed as I do. But just how, in these circumstances, does a fellow 'take it easy'? That's what I want to know."

"That," agrees the sponsor, "is a very good question indeed. I think I can tell you exactly how to relax. You won't have to work at it very hard, either. Listen, if you will, to these three statements. First, Alcoholics Anonymous does not demand that you believe anything. All of its Twelve Steps are but suggestions. Second, to get sober and to stay sober, you don't have to swallow all of Step Two right now. Looking back, I find that I took it piecemeal myself. Third, all you really need is a truly open mind. Just resign from the debating society and quit bothering yourself with such deep questions as whether it was the hen or the egg that came first. Again I say, all you need is the open mind."

The sponsor continues, "Take, for example, my own case. I had a scientific schooling. Naturally I respected, venerated, even worshiped science. As a matter of fact, I still do—all except the worship part. Time after time, my instructors held up to me the basic principle of all scientific progress: search and research, again and again, always with the open mind. When I first looked at A.A. my reaction was just like yours. This A.A. business, I thought, is totally unscientific. This I can't swallow. I simply won't consider such nonsense.

"Then I woke up. I had to admit that A.A. showed results, prodigious results. I saw that my attitude regarding these had been anything but scientific. It wasn't A.A. that had the closed mind, it was me. The minute I stopped arguing, I could begin to see and feel. Right there, Step Two gently and very gradually began to infiltrate my life. I can't say upon what occasion or upon what day I came to believe in a Power greater than myself, but I certainly have that belief now. To acquire it, I had only to stop fighting and practice the rest of A.A.'s program as enthusiastically as I could.

"This is only one man's opinion based on his own experience, of course. I must quickly assure you that A.A.'s tread innumerable paths in their quest for faith. If you don't care for the one I've suggested, you'll be sure to discover one that suits if only you look and listen. Many a man like you has begun to solve the problem by the method of substitution. You can, if you wish, make A.A. itself your 'higher power.' Here's a very large group of people who have solved their alcohol problem. In this respect they are certainly a power greater than you, who have not even come close to a solution. Surely you can have faith in them. Even this minimum of faith will be enough. You will find many members who have crossed the threshold just this way. All of them will tell you that, once across, their faith broadened and deepened. Relieved of the alcohol obsession, their lives un-accountably transformed, they came to believe in a Higher Power, and most of them began to talk of God."

Consider next the plight of those who once had faith, but have lost it. There will be those who have drifted into indifference, those filled with self-sufficiency who have cut themselves off, those who have become prejudiced against religion, and those who are downright defiant because God has failed to fulfill their demands. Can A.A. experience tell all these they may still find a faith that works?

Sometimes A.A. comes harder to those who have lost or rejected faith than to those who never had any faith at all, for they think they have tried faith and found it want-ing. They have tried the way of faith and the way of no faith. Since both ways have proved bitterly disappointing, they have concluded there is no place whatever for them to go. The roadblocks of indifference, fancied self-sufficiency, prejudice, and defiance often prove more solid and formi-dable for these people than any erected by the unconvinced agnostic or even the militant atheist. Religion says the ex-istence of God can be proved; the agnostic says it can't be proved; and the atheist claims proof of the nonexistence of God. Obviously, the dilemma of the wanderer from faith is that of profound confusion. He thinks himself lost to the comfort of any conviction at all. He cannot attain in even a small degree the assurance of the believer, the agnostic, or the atheist. He is the bewildered one.

Any number of A.A.'s can say to the drifter, "Yes, we were diverted from our childhood faith, too. The overcon-fidence of youth was too much for us. Of course, we were glad that good home and religious training had given us certain values. We were still sure that we ought to be fairly honest, tolerant, and just, that we ought to be ambitious and hardworking. We became convinced that such simple rules of fair play and decency would be enough.

"As material success founded upon no more than these ordinary attributes began to come to us, we felt we were winning at the game of life. This was exhilarating, and it made us happy. Why should we be bothered with theological abstractions and religious duties, or with the state of our souls here or hereafter? The here and now was good enough for us. The will to win would carry us through. But then alcohol began to have its way with us. Finally, when all our score cards read 'zero,' and we saw that one more strike would put us out of the game forever, we had to look for our lost faith. It was in A.A. that we rediscovered it. And so can you."

Now we come to another kind of problem: the intellectually self-sufficient man or woman. To these, many A.A.'s can say, "Yes, we were like you—far too smart for our own good. We loved to have people call us precocious. We used our education to blow ourselves up into prideful balloons, though we were careful to hide this from others. Secretly, we felt we could float above the rest of the folks on our brainpower alone. Scientific progress told us there was nothing man couldn't do. Knowledge was all-powerful. Intellect could conquer nature. Since we were brighter than most folks (so we thought), the spoils of victory would be ours for the thinking. The god of intellect displaced the God of our fathers. But again John Barleycorn had other ideas. We who had won so handsomely in a walk turned into all-time losers. We saw that we had to reconsider or die. We found many in A.A. who once thought as we did. They helped us to get down to our right size. By their example they showed us that humility and intellect could be compatible, provided we placed humility first. When we began to do that, we received the gift of faith, a faith which works. This faith is for you, too."

Another crowd of A.A.'s says: "We were plumb disgusted with religion and all its works. The Bible, we said, was full of nonsense; we could cite it chapter and verse, and we couldn't see the Beatitudes for the 'begats.' In spots its morality was impossibly good; in others it seemed impossibly bad. But it was the morality of the religionists themselves that really got us down. We gloated over the hypocrisy, bigotry, and crushing self-righteousness that clung to so many 'believers' even in their Sunday best. How we loved to shout the damaging fact that millions of the 'good men of religion' were still killing one another off in the name of God. This all meant, of course, that we had substituted negative for positive thinking. After we came to A.A., we had to recognize that this trait had been an ego-feeding proposition. In belaboring the sins of some religious people, we could feel superior to all of them. Moreover, we could avoid looking at some of our own shortcomings. Self-righteousness, the very thing that we had contemptuously condemned in others, was our own besetting evil. This phony form of respectability was our undoing, so far as faith was concerned. But finally, driven to A.A., we learned better.

"As psychiatrists have often observed, defiance is the outstanding characteristic of many an alcoholic. So it's not strange that lots of us have had our day at defying God Himself. Sometimes it's because God has not delivered us the good things of life which we specified, as a greedy child makes an impossible list for Santa Claus. More often, though, we had met up with some major calamity, and to our way of thinking lost out because God deserted us. The girl we wanted to marry had other notions; we prayed God that she'd change her mind, but she didn't. We prayed for healthy children, and were presented with sick ones, or none at all. We prayed for promotions at business, and none came. Loved ones, upon whom we heartily depended, were taken from us by so-called acts of God. Then we became drunkards, and asked God to stop that. But nothing happened. This was the unkindest cut of all. 'Damn this faith business!' we said.

"When we encountered A.A., the fallacy of our defiance was revealed. At no time had we asked what God's will was for us; instead we had been telling Him what it ought to be. No man, we saw, could believe in God and defy Him, too. Belief meant reliance, not defiance. In A.A. we saw the fruits of this belief: men and women spared from alcohol's final catastrophe. We saw them meet and transcend their other pains and trials. We saw them calmly accept impossible situations, seeking neither to run nor to recriminate. This was not only faith; it was faith that worked under all conditions. We soon concluded that whatever price in humility we must pay, we would pay."

Now let's take the guy full of faith, but still reeking of

alcohol. He believes he is devout. His religious observance is scrupulous. He's sure he still believes in God, but suspects that God doesn't believe in him. He takes pledges and more pledges. Following each, he not only drinks again, but acts worse than the last time. Valiantly he tries to fight alcohol, imploring God's help, but the help doesn't come. What, then, can be the matter?

To clergymen, doctors, friends, and families, the alcoholic who means well and tries hard is a heartbreaking riddle. To most A.A.'s, he is not. There are too many of us who have been just like him, and have found the riddle's answer. This answer has to do with the quality of faith rather than its quantity. This has been our blind spot. We supposed we had humility when really we hadn't. We supposed we had been serious about religious practices when, upon honest appraisal, we found we had been only superficial. Or, going to the other extreme, we had wallowed in emotionalism and had mistaken it for true religious feeling. In both cases, we had been asking something for nothing. The fact was we really hadn't cleaned house so that the grace of God could enter us and expel the obsession. In no deep or meaningful sense had we ever taken stock of ourselves, made amends to those we had harmed, or freely given to any other human being without any demand for reward. We had not even prayed rightly. We had always said, "Grant me my wishes" instead of "Thy will be done." The love of God and man we understood not at all. Therefore we remained self-deceived, and so incapable of receiving enough grace to restore us to sanity.

Few indeed are the practicing alcoholics who have any

idea how irrational they are, or seeing their irrationality, can bear to face it. Some will be willing to term themselves "problem drinkers," but cannot endure the suggestion that they are in fact mentally ill. They are abetted in this blindness by a world which does not understand the difference between sane drinking and alcoholism. "Sanity" is defined as "soundness of mind." Yet no alcoholic, soberly analyzing his destructive behavior, whether the destruction fell on the dining-room furniture or his own moral fiber, can claim "soundness of mind" for himself.

Therefore, Step Two is the rallying point for all of us. Whether agnostic, atheist, or former believer, we can stand together on this Step. True humility and an open mind can lead us to faith, and every A.A. meeting is an assurance that God will restore us to sanity if we rightly relate ourselves to Him.

Step Three

"Made a decision to turn our will and our lives over to the care of God __as we understood Him__."

PRACTICING Step Three is like the opening of a door which to all appearances is still closed and locked. All we need is a key, and the decision to swing the door open. There is only one key, and it is called willingness. Once unlocked by willingness, the door opens almost of itself, and looking through it, we shall see a pathway beside which is an inscription. It reads: "This is the way to a faith that works." In the first two Steps we were engaged in reflection. We saw that we were powerless over alcohol, but we also perceived that faith of some kind, if only in A.A. itself, is possible to anyone. These conclusions did not require action; they required only acceptance.

Like all the remaining Steps, Step Three calls for affirmative action, for it is only by action that we can cut away the self-will which has always blocked the entry of God—or, if you like, a Higher Power—into our lives. Faith, to be sure, is necessary, but faith alone can avail nothing. We can have faith, yet keep God out of our lives. Therefore our problem now becomes just how and by what specific means shall we be able to let Him in? Step Three represents our first attempt to do this. In fact, the effectiveness of the whole A.A. program will rest upon how well and earnestly we have tried to come to "a decision to turn our will and our lives over to the care of God *as we understood Him.*"

To every worldly and practical-minded beginner, this Step looks hard, even impossible. No matter how much one wishes to try, exactly how *can* he turn his own will and his own life over to the care of whatever God he thinks there is? Fortunately, we who have tried it, and with equal misgivings, can testify that anyone, anyone at all, can begin to do it. We can further add that a beginning, even the smallest, is all that is needed. Once we have placed the key of willingness in the lock and have the door ever so slightly open, we find that we can always open it some more. Though self-will may slam it shut again, as it frequently does, it will always respond the moment we again pick up the key of willingness.

Maybe this all sounds mysterious and remote, something like Einstein's theory of relativity or a proposition in nuclear physics. It isn't at all. Let's look at how practical it actually is. Every man and woman who has joined A.A. and intends to stick has, without realizing it, made a beginning on Step Three. Isn't it true that in all matters touching upon alcohol, each of them has decided to turn his or her life over to the care, protection, and guidance of Alcoholics Anonymous? Already a willingness has been achieved to cast out one's own will and one's own ideas about the alcohol problem in favor of those suggested by A.A. Any willing newcomer feels sure A.A. is the only safe harbor for the foundering vessel he has become. Now if this is not turning one's will and life over to a newfound Providence, then what is it?

But suppose that instinct still cries out, as it certainly will,

"Yes, respecting alcohol, I guess I have to be dependent upon A.A., but in all other matters I must still maintain my independence. Nothing is going to turn me into a nonentity. If I keep on turning my life and my will over to the care of Something or Somebody else, what will become of *me*? I'll look like the hole in the doughnut." This, of course, is the process by which instinct and logic always seek to bolster egotism, and so frustrate spiritual development. The trouble is that this kind of thinking takes no real account of the facts. And the facts seem to be these: The more we become willing to depend upon a Higher Power, the more independent we actually are. Therefore dependence, as A.A. practices it, is really a means of gaining true independence of the spirit.

Let's examine for a moment this idea of dependence at the level of everyday living. In this area it is startling to discover how dependent we really are, and how unconscious of that dependence. Every modern house has electric wiring carrying power and light to its interior. We are delighted with this dependence; our main hope is that nothing will ever cut off the supply of current. By so accepting our dependence upon this marvel of science, we find ourselves more independent personally. Not only are we more independent, we are even more comfortable and secure. Power flows just where it is needed. Silently and surely, electricity, that strange energy so few people understand, meets our simplest daily needs, and our most desperate ones, too. Ask the polio sufferer confined to an iron lung who depends with complete trust upon a motor to keep the breath of life in him.

But the moment our mental or emotional independence

is in question, how differently we behave. How persistently we claim the right to decide all by ourselves just what we shall think and just how we shall act. Oh yes, we'll weigh the pros and cons of every problem. We'll listen politely to those who would advise us, but all the decisions are to be ours alone. Nobody is going to meddle with our personal independence in such matters. Besides, we think, there is no one we can surely trust. We are certain that our intelligence, backed by willpower, can rightly control our inner lives and guarantee us success in the world we live in. This brave philosophy, wherein each man plays God, sounds good in the speaking, but it still has to meet the acid test: how well does it actually work? One good look in the mirror ought to be answer enough for any alcoholic.

Should his own image in the mirror be too awful to contemplate (and it usually is), he might first take a look at the results normal people are getting from self-sufficiency. Everywhere he sees people filled with anger and fear, society breaking up into warring fragments. Each fragment says to the others, "We are right and you are wrong." Every such pressure group, if it is strong enough, self-righteously imposes its will upon the rest. And everywhere the same thing is being done on an individual basis. The sum of all this mighty effort is less peace and less brotherhood than before. The philosophy of self-sufficiency is not paying off. Plainly enough, it is a bone-crushing juggernaut whose final achievement is ruin.

Therefore, we who are alcoholics can consider ourselves fortunate indeed. Each of us has had his own near-fatal encounter with the juggernaut of self-will, and has suffered enough under its weight to be willing to look for something better. So it is by circumstance rather than by any virtue that we have been driven to A.A., have admitted defeat, have acquired the rudiments of faith, and now want to make a decision to turn our will and our lives over to a Higher Power.

We realize that the word "dependence" is as distasteful to many psychiatrists and psychologists as it is to alcoholics. Like our professional friends, we, too, are aware that there are wrong forms of dependence. We have experienced many of them. No adult man or woman, for example, should be in too much emotional dependence upon a parent. They should have been weaned long before, and if they have not been, they should wake up to the fact. This very form of faulty dependence has caused many a rebellious alcoholic to conclude that dependence of any sort must be intolerably damaging. But dependence upon an A.A. group or upon a Higher Power hasn't produced any baleful results.

When World War II broke out, this spiritual principle had its first major test. A.A.'s entered the services and were scattered all over the world. Would they be able to take discipline, stand up under fire, and endure the monotony and misery of war? Would the kind of dependence they had learned in A.A. carry them through? Well, it did. They had even fewer alcoholic lapses or emotional binges than A.A.'s safe at home did. They were just as capable of endurance and valor as any other soldiers. Whether in Alaska or on the Salerno beachhead, their dependence upon a Higher Power worked. And far from being a weakness, this dependence was their chief source of strength.

So how, exactly, can the willing person continue to turn his will and his life over to the Higher Power? He made a beginning, we have seen, when he commenced to rely upon A.A. for the solution of his alcohol problem. By now, though, the chances are that he has become convinced that he has more problems than alcohol, and that some of these refuse to be solved by all the sheer personal determination and courage he can muster. They simply will not budge; they make him desperately unhappy and threaten his new-found sobriety. Our friend is still victimized by remorse and guilt when he thinks of yesterday. Bitterness still overpowers him when he broods upon those he still envies or hates. His financial insecurity worries him sick, and panic takes over when he thinks of all the bridges to safety that alcohol burned behind him. And how shall he ever straighten out that awful jam that cost him the affection of his family and separated him from them? His lone courage and unaided will cannot do it. Surely he must now depend upon Somebody or Something else.

At first that "somebody" is likely to be his closest A.A. friend. He relies upon the assurance that his many troubles, now made more acute because he cannot use alcohol to kill the pain, can be solved, too. Of course the sponsor points out that our friend's life is still unmanageable even though he is sober, that after all, only a bare start on A.A.'s program has been made. More sobriety brought about by the admission of alcoholism and by attendance at a few meetings is very good indeed, but it is bound to be a far cry from permanent sobriety and a contented, useful life.

That is just where the remaining Steps of the A.A. program come in. Nothing short of continuous action upon these as a way of life can bring the much-desired result.

Then it is explained that other Steps of the A.A. program can be practiced with success only when Step Three is given a determined and persistent trial. This statement may surprise newcomers who have experienced nothing but constant deflation and a growing conviction that human will is of no value whatever. They have become persuaded, and rightly so, that many problems besides alcohol will not yield to a headlong assault powered by the individual alone. But now it appears that there are certain things which only the individual can do. All by himself, and in the light of his own circumstances, he needs to develop the quality of willingness. When he acquires willingness, he is the only one who can make the decision to exert himself. Trying to do this is an act of his own will. All of the Twelve Steps require sustained and personal exertion to conform to their principles and so, we trust, to God's will.

It is when we try to make our will conform with God's that we begin to use it rightly. To all of us, this was a most wonderful revelation. *Our whole trouble had been the misuse of willpower. We had tried to bombard our problems with it instead of attempting to bring it into agreement with God's intention for us.* To make this increasingly possible is the purpose of A.A.'s Twelve Steps, and Step Three opens the door.

Once we have come into agreement with these ideas, it is really easy to begin the practice of Step Three. In all times of emotional disturbance or indecision, we can pause, ask for quiet, and in the stillness simply say: "God grant me the serenity to accept the things I cannot change, courage to change the things I can, and wisdom to know the difference. Thy will, not mine, be done."

Step Four

"Made a searching and fearless moral inventory of ourselves."

CREATION gave us instincts for a purpose. Without them we wouldn't be complete human beings. If men and women didn't exert themselves to be secure in their persons, made no effort to harvest food or construct shelter, there would be no survival. If they didn't reproduce, the earth wouldn't be populated. If there were no social instinct, if men cared nothing for the society of one another, there would be no society. So these desires—for the sex relation, for material and emotional security, and for companionship—are perfectly necessary and right, and surely God-given.

Yet these instincts, so necessary for our existence, often far exceed their proper functions. Powerfully, blindly, many times subtly, they drive us, dominate us, and insist upon ruling our lives. Our desires for sex, for material and emotional security, and for an important place in society often tyrannize us. When thus out of joint, man's natural desires cause him great trouble, practically all the trouble there is. No human being, however good, is exempt from these troubles. Nearly every serious emotional problem can be seen as a case of misdirected instinct. When that happens, our great natural assets, the instincts, have turned into physical and mental liabilities.

Step Four is our vigorous and painstaking effort to discover what these liabilities in each of us have been, and are.

We want to find exactly how, when, and where our natural desires have warped us. We wish to look squarely at the unhappiness this has caused others and ourselves. By discovering what our emotional deformities are, we can move toward their correction. Without a willing and persistent effort to do this, there can be little sobriety or contentment for us. Without a searching and fearless moral inventory, most of us have found that the faith which really works in daily living is still out of reach.

Before tackling the inventory problem in detail, let's have a closer look at what the basic problem is. Simple examples like the following take on a world of meaning when we think about them. Suppose a person places sex desire ahead of everything else. In such a case, this imperious urge can destroy his chances for material and emotional security as well as his standing in the community. Another may develop such an obsession for financial security that he wants to do nothing but hoard money. Going to the extreme, he can become a miser, or even a recluse who denies himself both family and friends.

Nor is the quest for security always expressed in terms of money. How frequently we see a frightened human being determined to depend completely upon a stronger person for guidance and protection. This weak one, failing to meet life's responsibilities with his own resources, never grows up. Disillusionment and helplessness are his lot. In time all his protectors either flee or die, and he is once more left alone and afraid.

We have also seen men and women who go power-mad,

who devote themselves to attempting to rule their fellows. These people often throw to the winds every chance for legitimate security and a happy family life. Whenever a human being becomes a battleground for the instincts, there can be no peace.

But that is not all of the danger. Every time a person imposes his instincts unreasonably upon others, unhappiness follows. If the pursuit of wealth tramples upon people who happen to be in the way, then anger, jealousy, and revenge are likely to be aroused. If sex runs riot, there is a similar uproar. Demands made upon other people for too much attention, protection, and love can only invite domination or revulsion in the protectors themselves—two emotions quite as unhealthy as the demands which evoked them. When an individual's desire for prestige becomes uncontrollable, whether in the sewing circle or at the international conference table, other people suffer and often revolt. This collision of instincts can produce anything from a cold snub to a blazing revolution. In these ways we are set in conflict not only with ourselves, but with other people who have instincts, too.

Alcoholics especially should be able to see that instinct run wild in themselves is the underlying cause of their destructive drinking. We have drunk to drown feelings of fear, frustration, and depression. We have drunk to escape the guilt of passions, and then have drunk again to make more passions possible. We have drunk for vainglory—that we might the more enjoy foolish dreams of pomp and power. This perverse soul-sickness is not pleasant to look upon. Instincts on rampage balk at investigation. The minute we make a serious attempt to probe them, we are liable to suffer severe reactions.

If temperamentally we are on the depressive side, we are apt to be swamped with guilt and self-loathing. We wallow in this messy bog, often getting a misshapen and painful pleasure out of it. As we morbidly pursue this melancholy activity, we may sink to such a point of despair that nothing but oblivion looks possible as a solution. Here, of course, we have lost all perspective, and therefore all genuine humility. For this is pride in reverse. This is not a moral inventory at all; it is the very process by which the depressive has so often been led to the bottle and extinction.

If, however, our natural disposition is inclined to self-righteousness or grandiosity, our reaction will be just the opposite. We will be offended at A.A.'s suggested inventory. No doubt we shall point with pride to the good lives we thought we led before the bottle cut us down. We shall claim that our serious character defects, if we think we have any at all, have been *caused* chiefly by excessive drinking. This being so, we think it logically follows that sobriety— first, last, and all the time—is the only thing we need to work for. We believe that our one-time good characters will be revived the moment we quit alcohol. If we were pretty nice people all along, except for our drinking, what need is there for a moral inventory now that we are sober?

We also clutch at another wonderful excuse for avoiding an inventory. Our present anxieties and troubles, we cry, are caused by the behavior of other people—people who *really* need a moral inventory. We firmly believe that if only they'd treat us better, we'd be all right. Therefore we think our indignation is justified and reasonable—that our resentments are the "right kind." *We* aren't the guilty ones. *They* are!

At this stage of the inventory proceedings, our sponsors come to the rescue. They can do this, for they are the carriers of A.A.'s tested experience with Step Four. They comfort the melancholy one by first showing him that his case is not strange or different, that his character defects are probably not more numerous or worse than those of anyone else in A.A. This the sponsor promptly proves by talking freely and easily, and without exhibitionism, about his own defects, past and present. This calm, yet realistic, stocktaking is immensely reassuring. The sponsor probably points out that the newcomer has some assets which can be noted along with his liabilities. This tends to clear away morbidity and encourage balance. As soon as he begins to be more objective, the newcomer can fearlessly, rather than fearfully, look at his own defects.

The sponsors of those who feel they need no inventory are confronted with quite another problem. This is because people who are driven by pride of self unconsciously blind themselves to their liabilities. These newcomers scarcely need comforting. The problem is to help them discover a chink in the walls their ego has built, through which the light of reason can shine.

First off, they can be told that the majority of A.A. members have suffered severely from self-justification during their drinking days. For most of us, self-justification was the maker of excuses; excuses, of course, for drinking, and for all kinds of crazy and damaging conduct. We had made the invention of alibis a fine art. We had to drink because times were hard or times were good. We had to drink because at home we were smothered with love or got none at all. We had to drink because at work we were great successes or dismal failures. We had to drink because our nation had won a war or lost a peace. And so it went, ad infinitum.

We thought "conditions" drove us to drink, and when we tried to correct these conditions and found that we couldn't to our entire satisfaction, our drinking went out of hand and we became alcoholics. It never occurred to us that we needed to change ourselves to meet conditions, whatever they were.

But in A.A. we slowly learned that something had to be done about our vengeful resentments, self-pity, and unwarranted pride. We had to see that every time we played the big shot, we turned people against us. We had to see that when we harbored grudges and planned revenge for such defeats, we were really beating ourselves with the club of anger we had intended to use on others. We learned that if we were seriously disturbed, our *first* need was to quiet that disturbance, regardless of who or what we thought caused it.

To see how erratic emotions victimized us often took a long time. We could perceive them quickly in others, but only slowly in ourselves. First of all, we had to admit that we had many of these defects, even though such disclosures were painful and humiliating. Where other people were concerned, we had to drop the word "blame" from our speech and thought. This required great willingness even to begin. But once over the first two or three high hurdles, the course ahead began to look easier. For we had started to get perspective on ourselves, which is another way of saying that we were gaining in humility.

Of course the depressive and the power-driver are personality extremes, types with which A.A. and the whole world abound. Often these personalities are just as sharply defined as the examples given. But just as often some of us will fit more or less into both classifications. Human beings are never quite alike, so each of us, when making an inventory, will need to determine what his individual character defects are. Having found the shoes that fit, he ought to step into them and walk with new confidence that he is at last on the right track.

Now let's ponder the need for a list of the more glaring personality defects all of us have in varying degrees. To those having religious training, such a list would set forth serious violations of moral principles. Some others will think of this list as defects of character. Still others will call it an index of maladjustments. Some will become quite annoyed if there is talk about immorality, let alone sin. But all who are in the least reasonable will agree upon one point: that there is plenty wrong with us alcoholics about which plenty will have to be done if we are to expect sobriety, progress, and any real ability to cope with life.

To avoid falling into confusion over the names these defects should be called, let's take a universally recognized list of major human failings—the Seven Deadly Sins of pride, greed, lust, anger, gluttony, envy, and sloth. It is not by accident that pride heads the procession. For pride, lead-ing to self-justification, and always spurred by conscious or unconscious fears, is the basic breeder of most human difficulties, the chief block to true progress. Pride lures us into making demands upon ourselves or upon others which cannot be met without perverting or misusing our God-given instincts. When the satisfaction of our instincts for sex, security, and society becomes the sole object of our lives, then pride steps in to justify our excesses.

All these failings generate fear, a soul-sickness in its own right. Then fear, in turn, generates more character defects. Unreasonable fear that our instincts will not be satisfied drives us to covet the possessions of others, to lust for sex and power, to become angry when our instinctive demands are threatened, to be envious when the ambitions of others seem to be realized while ours are not. We eat, drink, and grab for more of everything than we need, fearing we shall never have enough. And with genuine alarm at the prospect of work, we stay lazy. We loaf and procrastinate, or at best work grudgingly and under half steam. These fears are the termites that ceaselessly devour the foundations of whatever sort of life we try to build.

So when A.A. suggests a fearless moral inventory, it must seem to every newcomer that more is being asked of him than he can do. Both his pride and his fear beat him back every time he tries to look within himself. Pride says, "You need not pass this way," and Fear says, "You dare not look!" But the testimony of A.A.'s who have really tried a moral inventory is that pride and fear of this sort turn out to be bogeymen, nothing else. Once we have a complete willingness to take inventory, and exert ourselves to do the job thoroughly, a wonderful light falls upon this foggy scene. As we persist, a brand-new kind of confidence is born, and the sense of relief at finally facing ourselves is indescribable. These are the first fruits of Step Four.

By now the newcomer has probably arrived at the following conclusions: that his character defects, representing instincts gone astray, have been the primary cause of his drinking and his failure at life; that unless he is now willing to work hard at the elimination of the worst of these defects, both sobriety and peace of mind will still elude him; that all the faulty foundation of his life will have to be torn out and built anew on bedrock. Now willing to commence the search for his own defects, he will ask, "Just how do I go about this? *How* do I take inventory of myself?"

Since Step Four is but the beginning of a lifetime practice, it can be suggested that he first have a look at those personal flaws which are acutely troublesome and fairly obvious. Using his best judgment of what has been right and what has been wrong, he might make a rough survey of his conduct with respect to his primary instincts for sex, security, and society. Looking back over his life, he can readily get under way by consideration of questions such as these:

When, and how, and in just what instances did my selfish pursuit of the sex relation damage other people and me? What people were hurt, and how badly? Did I spoil my marriage and injure my children? Did I jeopardize my standing in the community? Just how did I react to these situations at the time? Did I burn with a guilt that nothing could extinguish? Or did I insist that I was the pursued and not the pursuer, and thus absolve myself? How have I reacted to frustration in sexual matters? When denied, did I become vengeful or depressed? Did I take it out on other people? If there was rejection or coldness at home, did I use this as a reason for promiscuity?

Also of importance for most alcoholics are the questions they must ask about their behavior respecting financial and emotional security. In these areas fear, greed, possessiveness, and pride have too often done their worst. Surveying his business or employment record, almost any alcoholic can ask questions like these: In addition to my drinking problem, what character defects contributed to my financial instability? Did fear and inferiority about my fitness for my job destroy my confidence and fill me with conflict? Did I try to cover up those feelings of inadequacy by bluffing, cheating, lying, or evading responsibility? Or by griping that others failed to recognize my truly exceptional abilities? Did I overvalue myself and play the big shot? Did I have such unprincipled ambition that I double-crossed and undercut my associates? Was I extravagant? Did I recklessly borrow money, caring little whether it was repaid or not? Was I a pinchpenny, refusing to support my family properly? Did I cut corners financially? What about the "quick money" deals, the stock market, and the races?

Businesswomen in A.A. will naturally find that many of these questions apply to them, too. But the alcoholic housewife can also make the family financially insecure. She can juggle charge accounts, manipulate the food budget, spend her afternoons gambling, and run her husband into debt by irresponsibility, waste, and extravagance.

But all alcoholics who have drunk themselves out of jobs, family, and friends will need to cross-examine themselves ruthlessly to determine how their own personality defects have thus demolished their security.

The most common symptoms of emotional insecurity are worry, anger, self-pity, and depression. These stem from causes which sometimes seem to be within us, and at other times to come from without. To take inventory in this respect we ought to consider carefully all personal relationships which bring continuous or recurring trouble. It should be remembered that this kind of insecurity may arise in any area where instincts are threatened. Questioning directed to this end might run like this: Looking at both past and present, what sex situations have caused me anxiety, bitterness, frustration, or depression? Appraising each situation fairly, can I see where I have been at fault? Did these perplexities beset me because of selfishness or unreasonable demands? Or, if my disturbance was seemingly caused by the behavior of others, why do I lack the ability to accept conditions I cannot change? These are the sort of fundamental inquiries that can disclose the source of my discomfort and indicate whether I may be able to alter my own conduct and so adjust myself serenely to self-discipline.

Suppose that financial insecurity constantly arouses these same feelings. I can ask myself to what extent have my own mistakes fed my gnawing anxieties. And if the actions of others are part of the cause, what can I do about that? If I am unable to change the present state of affairs, am I willing to take the measures necessary to shape my life to conditions as they are? Questions like these, more of which will come to mind easily in each individual case, will help turn up the root causes.

But it is from our twisted relations with family, friends, and society at large that many of us have suffered the most. We have been especially stupid and stubborn about them. The primary fact that we fail to recognize is our total inability to form a true partnership with another human being. Our egomania digs two disastrous pitfalls. Either we insist upon dominating the people we know, or we depend upon them far too much. If we lean too heavily on people, they will sooner or later fail us, for they are human, too, and cannot possibly meet our incessant demands. In this way our insecurity grows and festers. When we habitually try to manipulate others to our own willful desires, they revolt, and resist us heavily. Then we develop hurt feelings, a sense of persecution, and a desire to retaliate. As we redouble our efforts at control, and continue to fail, our suffering becomes acute and constant. We have not once sought to be one in a family, to be a friend among friends, to be a worker among workers, to be a useful member of society. Always we tried to struggle to the top of the heap, or to hide underneath it. This self-centered behavior blocked a partnership relation with any one of those about us. Of true brotherhood we had small comprehension.

Some will object to many of the questions posed, because they think their own character defects have not been so glaring. To these it can be suggested that a conscientious examination is likely to reveal the very defects the objectionable questions are concerned with. Because our surface record hasn't looked too bad, we have frequently been abashed to find that this is so simply because we have buried these selfsame defects deep down in us under thick layers of self-justification. Whatever the defects, they have finally ambushed us into alcoholism and misery.

Therefore, thoroughness ought to be the watchword when taking inventory. In this connection, it is wise to write out our questions and answers. It will be an aid to clear thinking and honest appraisal. It will be the first *tangible* evidence of our complete willingness to move forward.

Step Five

"Admitted to God, to ourselves, and to another human being the exact nature of our wrongs."

ALL of A.A.'s Twelve Steps ask us to go contrary to our natural desires ... they all deflate our egos. When it comes to ego deflation, few Steps are harder to take than Five. But scarcely any Step is more necessary to longtime sobriety and peace of mind than this one.

A.A. experience has taught us we cannot live alone with our pressing problems and the character defects which cause or aggravate them. If we have swept the searchlight of Step Four back and forth over our careers, and it has revealed in stark relief those experiences we'd rather not remember, if we have come to know how wrong thinking and action have hurt us and others, then the need to quit living by ourselves with those tormenting ghosts of yesterday gets more urgent than ever. We have to talk to somebody about them.

So intense, though, is our fear and reluctance to do this, that many A.A.'s at first try to bypass Step Five. We search for an easier way—which usually consists of the general and fairly painless admission that when drinking we were sometimes bad actors. Then, for good measure, we add dramatic descriptions of that part of our drinking behavior which our friends probably know about anyhow.

But of the things which really bother and burn us, we

say nothing. Certain distressing or humiliating memories, we tell ourselves, ought not be shared with anyone. These will remain our secret. Not a soul must ever know. We hope they'll go to the grave with us.

Yet if A.A.'s experience means anything at all, this is not only unwise, but is actually a perilous resolve. Few muddled attitudes have caused us more trouble than holding back on Step Five. Some people are unable to stay sober at all; others will relapse periodically until they really clean house. Even A.A. oldtimers, sober for years, often pay dearly for skimping this Step. They will tell how they tried to carry the load alone; how much they suffered of irritability, anxiety, remorse, and depression; and how, unconsciously seeking relief, they would sometimes accuse even their best friends of the very character defects they themselves were trying to conceal. They always discovered that relief never came by confessing the sins of other people. Everybody had to confess his own.

This practice of admitting one's defects to another person is, of course, very ancient. It has been validated in every century, and it characterizes the lives of all spiritually centered and truly religious people. But today religion is by no means the sole advocate of this saving principle. Psychiatrists and psychologists point out the deep need every human being has for practical insight and knowledge of his own personality flaws and for a discussion of them with an understanding and trustworthy person. So far as alcoholics are concerned, A.A. would go even further. Most of us would declare that without a fearless admission of our defects to another human being we could not stay sober. It seems plain that the grace of God will not enter to expel our destructive obsessions until we are willing to try this.

What are we likely to receive from Step Five? For one thing, we shall get rid of that terrible sense of isolation we've always had. Almost without exception, alcoholics are tortured by loneliness. Even before our drinking got bad and people began to cut us off, nearly all of us suffered the feeling that we didn't quite belong. Either we were shy, and dared not draw near others, or we were apt to be noisy good fellows craving attention and companionship, but never getting it—at least to our way of thinking. There was always that mysterious barrier we could neither surmount nor understand. It was as if we were actors on a stage, suddenly realizing that we did not know a single line of our parts. That's one reason we loved alcohol too well. It did let us act extemporaneously. But even Bacchus boomeranged on us; we were finally struck down and left in terrified loneliness.

When we reached A.A., and for the first time in our lives stood among people who seemed to understand, the sense of belonging was tremendously exciting. We thought the isolation problem had been solved. But we soon discovered that while we weren't alone any more in a social sense, we still suffered many of the old pangs of anxious apartness. Until we had talked with complete candor of our conflicts, and had listened to someone else do the same thing, we still didn't belong. Step Five was the answer. It was the beginning of true kinship with man and God.

This vital Step was also the means by which we began to

get the feeling that we could be forgiven, no matter what we had thought or done. Often it was while working on this Step with our sponsors or spiritual advisers that we first felt truly able to forgive others, no matter how deeply we felt they had wronged us. Our moral inventory had persuaded us that all-round forgiveness was desirable, but it was only when we resolutely tackled Step Five that we inwardly *knew* we'd be able to receive forgiveness and give it, too.

Another great dividend we may expect from confiding our defects to another human being is humility—a word often misunderstood. To those who have made progress in A.A., it amounts to a clear recognition of what and who we really are, followed by a sincere attempt to become what we could be. Therefore, our first practical move toward humility must consist of recognizing our deficiencies. No defect can be corrected unless we clearly see what it is. But we shall have to do more than *see*. The objective look at ourselves we achieved in Step Four was, after all, only a look. All of us saw, for example, that we lacked honesty and tolerance, that we were beset at times by attacks of self-pity or delusions of personal grandeur. But while this was a humiliating experience, it didn't necessarily mean that we had yet acquired much actual humility. Though now recognized, our defects were still there. Something had to be done about them. And we soon found that we could not wish or will them away by ourselves.

More realism and therefore more honesty about ourselves are the great gains we make under the influence of

Step Five. As we took inventory, we began to suspect how much trouble self-delusion had been causing us. This had brought a disturbing reflection. If all our lives we had more or less fooled ourselves, how could we now be so sure that we weren't still self-deceived? How could we be certain that we had made a true catalog of our defects and had really admitted them, even to ourselves? Because we were still bothered by fear, self-pity, and hurt feelings, it was probable we couldn't appraise ourselves fairly at all. Too much guilt and remorse might cause us to dramatize and exaggerate our shortcomings. Or anger and hurt pride might be the smoke screen under which we were hiding some of our defects while we blamed others for them. Possibly, too, we were still handicapped by many liabilities, great and small, we never knew we had.

Hence it was most evident that a solitary self-appraisal, and the admission of our defects based upon that alone, wouldn't be nearly enough. We'd have to have outside help if we were surely to know and admit the truth about ourselves—the help of God and another human being. Only by discussing ourselves, holding back nothing, only by being willing to take advice and accept direction could we set foot on the road to straight thinking, solid honesty, and genuine humility.

Yet many of us still hung back. We said, "Why can't 'God as we understand Him' tell us where we are astray? If the Creator gave us our lives in the first place, then He must know in every detail where we have since gone wrong. Why don't we make our admissions to Him directly? Why do we need to bring anyone else into this?"

At this stage, the difficulties of trying to deal rightly

with God by ourselves are twofold. Though we may at first
be startled to realize that God knows all about us, we are
apt to get used to that quite quickly. Somehow, being alone
with God doesn't seem as embarrassing as facing up to another person. Until we actually sit down and talk aloud
about what we have so long hidden, our willingness to
clean house is still largely theoretical. When we are honest
with another person, it confirms that we have been honest
with ourselves and with God.

The second difficulty is this: what comes to us alone may
be garbled by our own rationalization and wishful thinking.
The benefit of talking to another person is that we can get
his direct comment and counsel on our situation, and there
can be no doubt in our minds what that advice is. Going it
alone in spiritual matters is dangerous. How many times
have we heard well-intentioned people claim the guidance
of God when it was all too plain that they were sorely mistaken. Lacking both practice and humility, they had delud-
ed themselves and were able to justify the most arrant nonsense on the ground that this was what God had told them.
It is worth noting that people of very high spiritual development almost always insist on checking with friends or spiritual advisers the guidance they feel they have received from
God. Surely, then, a novice ought not lay himself open to
the chance of making foolish, perhaps tragic, blunders in
this fashion. While the comment or advice of others may be
by no means infallible, it is likely to be far more specific
than any direct guidance we may receive while we are still so
inexperienced in establishing contact with a Power greater
than ourselves.

Our next problem will be to discover the person in whom we are to confide. Here we ought to take much care, remembering that prudence is a virtue which carries a high rating. Perhaps we shall need to share with this person facts about ourselves which no others ought to know. We shall want to speak with someone who is experienced, who not only has stayed dry but has been able to surmount other serious difficulties. Difficulties, perhaps, like our own. This person may turn out to be one's sponsor, but not necessarily so. If you have developed a high confidence in him, and his temperament and problems are close to your own, then such a choice will be good. Besides, your sponsor already has the advantage of knowing something about your case.

Perhaps, though, your relation to him is such that you would care to reveal only a part of your story. If this is the situation, by all means do so, for you ought to make a beginning as soon as you can. It may turn out, however, that you'll choose someone else for the more difficult and deeper revelations. This individual may be entirely outside of A.A. —for example, your clergyman or your doctor. For some of us, a complete stranger may prove the best bet.

The real tests of the situation are your own willingness to confide and your full confidence in the one with whom you share your first accurate self-survey. Even when you've found the person, it frequently takes great resolution to approach him or her. No one ought to say the A.A. program requires no willpower; here is one place you may require all you've got. Happily, though, the chances are that you will be in for a very pleasant surprise. When your mission is carefully explained, and it is seen by the recipient of your confidence how helpful he can really be, the conversation will start easily and will soon become eager. Before long, your listener may well tell a story or two about himself which will place you even more at ease. Provided you hold back nothing, your sense of relief will mount from minute to minute. The dammed-up emotions of years break out of their confinement, and miraculously vanish as soon as they are exposed. As the pain subsides, a healing tranquillity takes its place. And when humility and serenity are so combined, something else of great moment is apt to occur. Many an A.A., once agnostic or atheistic, tells us that it was during this stage of Step Five that he first actually felt the presence of God. And even those who had faith already often become conscious of God as they never were before.

This feeling of being at one with God and man, this emerging from isolation through the open and honest sharing of our terrible burden of guilt, brings us to a resting place where we may prepare ourselves for the following Steps toward a full and meaningful sobriety.

Step Six

"Were entirely ready to have God remove all these defects of character."

"THIS is the Step that separates the men from the boys." So declares a well-loved clergyman who happens to be one of A.A.'s greatest friends. He goes on to explain that any person capable of enough willingness and honesty to try repeatedly Step Six on all his faults—*without any reservations whatever*—has indeed come a long way spiritually, and is therefore entitled to be called a man who is sincerely trying to grow in the image and likeness of his own Creator.

Of course, the often disputed question of whether God can—and will, under certain conditions—remove defects of character will be answered with a prompt affirmative by almost any A.A. member. To him, this proposition will be no theory at all; it will be just about the largest fact in his life. He will usually offer his proof in a statement like this:

"Sure, I was beaten, absolutely licked. My own will-power just wouldn't work on alcohol. Change of scene, the best efforts of family, friends, doctors, and clergymen got no place with my alcoholism. I simply couldn't stop drinking, and no human being could seem to do the job for me. But when I became willing to clean house and then asked a Higher Power, God as I understood Him, to give me release, my obsession to drink vanished. It was lifted right out of me."

In A.A. meetings all over the world, statements just like this are heard daily. It is plain for everybody to see that each sober A.A. member has been granted a release from this very obstinate and potentially fatal obsession. So in a very complete and literal way, all A.A.'s have "become entirely ready" to have God remove the mania for alcohol from their lives. And God has proceeded to do exactly that.

Having been granted a perfect release from alcoholism, why then shouldn't we be able to achieve by the same means a perfect release from every other difficulty or defect? This is a riddle of our existence, the full answer to which may be only in the mind of God. Nevertheless, at least a part of the answer to it is apparent to us.

When men and women pour so much alcohol into themselves that they destroy their lives, they commit a most unnatural act. Defying their instinctive desire for self-preservation, they seem bent upon self-destruction. They work against their own deepest instinct. As they are humbled by the terrific beating administered by alcohol, the grace of God can enter them and expel their obsession. Here their powerful instinct to live can cooperate fully with their Creator's desire to give them new life. For nature and God alike abhor suicide.

But most of our other difficulties don't fall under such a category at all. Every normal person wants, for example, to eat, to reproduce, to be somebody in the society of his fellows. And he wishes to be reasonably safe and secure as he tries to attain these things. Indeed, God made him that way. He did not design man to destroy himself by alcohol, but He did give man instincts to help him to stay alive.

It is nowhere evident, at least in this life, that our Creator expects us fully to eliminate our instinctual drives. So far as we know, it is nowhere on the record that God has completely removed from any human being all his natural drives.

Since most of us are born with an abundance of natural desires, it isn't strange that we often let these far exceed their intended purpose. When they drive us blindly, or we willfully demand that they supply us with more satisfactions or pleasures than are possible or due us, that is the point at which we depart from the degree of perfection that God wishes for us here on earth. That is the measure of our character defects, or, if you wish, of our sins.

If we ask, God will certainly forgive our derelictions. But in no case does He render us white as snow and keep us that way without our cooperation. That is something we are supposed to be willing to work toward ourselves. He asks only that we try as best we know how to make progress in the building of character.

So Step Six—"Were entirely ready to have God remove all these defects of character"—is A.A.'s way of stating the best possible attitude one can take in order to make a beginning on this lifetime job. This does not mean that we expect all our character defects to be lifted out of us as the drive to drink was. A few of them may be, but with most of them we shall have to be content with patient improvement. The key words "entirely ready" underline the fact that we want to aim at the very best we know or can learn.

How many of us have this degree of readiness? In an absolute sense practically nobody has it. The best we can do, with all the honesty that we can summon, is to *try* to have it. Even then the best of us will discover to our dismay that there is always a sticking point, a point at which we say, "No, I can't give this up yet." And we shall often tread on even more dangerous ground when we cry, "This I will *never* give up!" Such is the power of our instincts to overreach themselves. No matter how far we have progressed, desires will always be found which oppose the grace of God.

Some who feel they have done well may dispute this, so let's try to think it through a little further. Practically everybody wishes to be rid of his most glaring and destructive handicaps. No one wants to be so proud that he is scorned as a braggart, nor so greedy that he is labeled a thief. No one wants to be angry enough to murder, lustful enough to rape, gluttonous enough to ruin his health. No one wants to be agonized by the chronic pain of envy or to be paralyzed by sloth. Of course, most human beings don't suffer these defects at these rock-bottom levels.

We who have escaped these extremes are apt to congratulate ourselves. Yet can we? After all, hasn't it been self-interest, pure and simple, that has enabled most of us to escape? Not much spiritual effort is involved in avoiding excesses which will bring us punishment anyway. But when we face up to the less violent aspects of these very same defects, *then* where do we stand?

What we must recognize now is that we exult in some of our defects. We really love them. Who, for example, doesn't like to feel just a little superior to the next fellow, or even quite a lot superior? Isn't it true that we like to let greed masquerade as ambition? To think of *liking* lust seems impossible. But how many men and women speak love with their lips, and believe what they say, so that they can hide lust in a dark corner of their minds? And even while staying within conventional bounds, many people have to admit that their imaginary sex excursions are apt to be all dressed up as dreams of romance.

Self-righteous anger also can be very enjoyable. In a perverse way we can actually take satisfaction from the fact that many people annoy us, for it brings a comfortable feeling of superiority. Gossip barbed with our anger, a polite form of murder by character assassination, has its satisfactions for us, too. Here we are not trying to help those we criticize; we are trying to proclaim our own righteousness.

When gluttony is less than ruinous, we have a milder word for that, too; we call it "taking our comfort." We live in a world riddled with envy. To a greater or less degree, everybody is infected with it. From this defect we must surely get a warped yet definite satisfaction. Else why would we consume such great amounts of time wishing for what we have not, rather than working for it, or angrily looking for attributes we shall never have, instead of adjusting to the fact, and accepting it? And how often we work hard with no better motive than to be secure and slothful later on—only we call that "retiring." Consider, too, our talents for procrastination, which is really sloth in five syllables. Nearly anyone could submit a good list of such defects as these, and few of us would seriously think of giving them up, at least until they cause us excessive misery.

Some people, of course, may conclude that they are indeed ready to have all such defects taken from them. But even these people, if they construct a list of still milder defects, will be obliged to admit that they prefer to hang on to *some* of them. Therefore, it seems plain that few of us can quickly or easily become ready to aim at spiritual and moral perfection; we want to settle for only as much perfection as will get us by in life, according, of course, to our various and sundry ideas of what will get us by. So the difference between "the boys and the men" is the difference between striving for a self-determined objective and for the perfect objective which is of God.

Many will at once ask, "How *can* we accept the entire implication of Step Six? Why—that is *perfection*!" This sounds like a hard question, but practically speaking, it isn't. Only Step One, where we made the 100 percent admission we were powerless over alcohol, can be practiced with absolute perfection. The remaining eleven Steps state perfect ideals. They are goals toward which we look, and the measuring sticks by which we estimate our progress. Seen in this light, Step Six is still difficult, but not at all impossible. The only urgent thing is that we make a beginning, and keep trying.

If we would gain any real advantage in the use of this Step on problems other than alcohol, we shall need to make a brand new venture into open-mindedness. We shall need to raise our eyes toward perfection, and be ready to walk in that direction. It will seldom matter how haltingly we walk. The only question will be "Are we ready?"

Looking again at those defects we are still unwilling to give up, we ought to erase the hard-and-fast lines that we have drawn. Perhaps we shall be obliged in some cases still to say, "This I cannot give up yet…," but we should not say to ourselves, "This I will *never* give up!"

Let's dispose of what appears to be a hazardous open end we have left. It is suggested that we ought to become entirely willing to aim toward perfection. We note that some delay, however, might be pardoned. That word, in the mind of a rationalizing alcoholic, could certainly be given a long-term meaning. He could say, "How very easy! Sure, I'll head toward perfection, but I'm certainly not going to hurry any. Maybe I can postpone dealing with some of my problems indefinitely." Of course, this won't do. Such a bluffing of oneself will have to go the way of many another pleasant rationalization. At the very least, we shall have to come to grips with some of our worst character defects and take action toward their removal as quickly as we can.

The moment we say, "No, never!" our minds close against the grace of God. Delay is dangerous, and rebellion may be fatal. This is the exact point at which we abandon limited objectives, and move toward God's will for us.

Step Seven

"Humbly asked Him to remove our shortcomings."

SINCE this Step so specifically concerns itself with humility, we should pause here to consider what humility is and what the practice of it can mean to us.

Indeed, the attainment of greater humility is the foundation principle of each of A.A.'s Twelve Steps. For without some degree of humility, no alcoholic can stay sober at all. Nearly all A.A.'s have found, too, that unless they develop much more of this precious quality than may be required just for sobriety, they still haven't much chance of becoming truly happy. Without it, they cannot live to much useful purpose, or, in adversity, be able to summon the faith that can meet any emergency.

Humility, as a word and as an ideal, has a very bad time of it in our world. Not only is the idea misunderstood; the word itself is often intensely disliked. Many people haven't even a nodding acquaintance with humility as a way of life. Much of the everyday talk we hear, and a great deal of what we read, highlights man's pride in his own achievements.

With great intelligence, men of science have been forcing nature to disclose her secrets. The immense resources now being harnessed promise such a quantity of material blessings that many have come to believe that a man-made millennium lies just ahead. Poverty will disappear, and there will be such abundance that everybody can have all the security and personal satisfactions he desires. The theory seems to be that once everybody's primary instincts are satisfied, there won't be much left to quarrel about. The world will then turn happy and be free to concentrate on culture and character. Solely by their own intelligence and labor, men will have shaped their own destiny.

Certainly no alcoholic, and surely no member of A.A., wants to deprecate material achievement. Nor do we enter into debate with the many who still so passionately cling to the belief that to satisfy our basic natural desires is the main object of life. But we *are* sure that no class of people in the world ever made a worse mess of trying to live by this formula than alcoholics. For thousands of years we have been demanding more than our share of security, prestige, and romance. When we seemed to be succeeding, we drank to dream still greater dreams. When we were frustrated, even in part, we drank for oblivion. Never was there enough of what we thought we wanted.

In all these strivings, so many of them well-intentioned, our crippling handicap had been our lack of humility. We had lacked the perspective to see that character-building and spiritual values had to come first, and that material satisfactions were not the purpose of living. Quite characteristically, we had gone all out in confusing the ends with the means. Instead of regarding the satisfaction of our material desires as the means by which we could live and function as human beings, we had taken these satisfactions to be the final end and aim of life.

True, most of us thought good character was desirable,

but obviously good character was something one needed to get on with the business of being self-satisfied. With a proper display of honesty and morality, we'd stand a better chance of getting what we really wanted. But whenever we had to choose between character and comfort, the character-building was lost in the dust of our chase after what we thought was happiness. Seldom did we look at character-building as something desirable in itself, something we would like to strive for whether our instinctual needs were met or not. We never thought of making honesty, tolerance, and true love of man and God the daily basis of living.

This lack of anchorage to any permanent values, this blindness to the true purpose of our lives, produced another bad result. For just so long as we were convinced that we could live exclusively by our own individual strength and intelligence, for just that long was a working faith in a Higher Power impossible. This was true even when we believed that God existed. We could actually have earnest religious beliefs which remained barren because we were still trying to play God ourselves. As long as we placed self-reliance first, a genuine reliance upon a Higher Power was out of the question. That basic ingredient of all humility, a desire to seek and do God's will, was missing.

For us, the process of gaining a new perspective was unbelievably painful. It was only by repeated humiliations that we were forced to learn something about humility. It was only at the end of a long road, marked by successive defeats and humiliations, and the final crushing of our self-sufficiency, that we began to feel humility as something more than a condition of groveling despair. Every newcomer in Alcoholics Anonymous is told, and soon realizes for himself, that his humble admission of powerlessness over alcohol is his first step toward liberation from its paralyzing grip.

So it is that we first see humility as a necessity. But this is the barest beginning. To get completely away from our aversion to the idea of being humble, to gain a vision of humility as the avenue to true freedom of the human spirit, to be willing to work for humility as something to be desired for itself, takes most of us a long, long time. A whole lifetime geared to self-centeredness cannot be set in reverse all at once. Rebellion dogs our every step at first.

When we have finally admitted without reservation that we are powerless over alcohol, we are apt to breathe a great sigh of relief, saying, "Well, thank God that's over! I'll never have to go through *that* again!" Then we learn, often to our consternation, that this is only the first milestone on the new road we are walking. Still goaded by sheer necessity, we reluctantly come to grips with those serious character flaws that made problem drinkers of us in the first place, flaws which must be dealt with to prevent a retreat into alcoholism once again. We will want to be rid of some of these defects, but in some instances this will appear to be an impossible job from which we recoil. And we cling with a passionate persistence to others which are just as disturbing to our equilibrium, because we still enjoy them too much. How can we possibly summon the resolution and the willingness to get rid of such overwhelming compulsions and desires?

But again we are driven on by the inescapable conclusion which we draw from A.A. experience, that we surely must try with a will, or else fall by the wayside. At this stage of our progress we are under heavy pressure and coercion to do the right thing. We are obliged to choose between the pains of trying and the certain penalties of failing to do so. These initial steps along the road are taken grudgingly, yet we do take them. We may still have no very high opinion of humility as a desirable personal virtue, but we do recognize it as a necessary aid to our survival.

But when we have taken a square look at some of these defects, have discussed them with another, and have become willing to have them removed, our thinking about humility commences to have a wider meaning. By this time in all probability we have gained some measure of release from our more devastating handicaps. We enjoy moments in which there is something like real peace of mind. To those of us who have hitherto known only excitement, depression, or anxiety—in other words, to all of us—this newfound peace is a priceless gift. Something new indeed has been added. Where humility had formerly stood for a forced feeding on humble pie, it now begins to mean the nourishing ingredient which can give us serenity.

This improved perception of humility starts another revolutionary change in our outlook. Our eyes begin to open to the immense values which have come straight out of painful ego-puncturing. Until now, our lives have been largely devoted to running from pain and problems. We fled from them as from a plague. We never wanted to deal with the fact of suffering. Escape via the bottle was always our solution. Character-building through suffering might be all right for saints, but it certainly didn't appeal to us.

Then, in A.A., we looked and listened. Everywhere we saw failure and misery transformed by humility into priceless assets. We heard story after story of how humility had brought strength out of weakness. In every case, pain had been the price of admission into a new life. But this admission price had purchased more than we expected. It brought a measure of humility, which we soon discovered to be a healer of pain. We began to fear pain less, and desire humility more than ever.

During this process of learning more about humility, the most profound result of all was the change in our attitude toward God. And this was true whether we had been believers or unbelievers. We began to get over the idea that the Higher Power was a sort of bush-league pinch hitter, to be called upon only in an emergency. The notion that we would still live our own lives, God helping a little now and then, began to evaporate. Many of us who had thought ourselves religious awoke to the limitations of this attitude. Refusing to place God first, we had deprived ourselves of His help. But now the words "Of myself I am nothing, the Father doeth the works" began to carry bright promise and meaning.

We saw we needn't always be bludgeoned and beaten into humility. It could come quite as much from our voluntary reaching for it as it could from unremitting suffering. A great turning point in our lives came when we sought for humility as something we really wanted, rather than as something we *must* have. It marked the time when we could commence to see the full implication of Step Seven: "Humbly asked Him to remove our shortcomings."

As we approach the actual taking of Step Seven, it might be well if we A.A.'s inquire once more just what our deeper objectives are. Each of us would like to live at peace with himself and with his fellows. We would like to be assured that the grace of God can do for us what we cannot do for ourselves. We have seen that character defects based upon shortsighted or unworthy desires are the obstacles that block our path toward these objectives. We now clearly see that we have been making unreasonable demands upon ourselves, upon others, and upon God.

The chief activator of our defects has been self-centered fear—primarily fear that we would lose something we already possessed or would fail to get something we demanded. Living upon a basis of unsatisfied demands, we were in a state of continual disturbance and frustration. Therefore, no peace was to be had unless we could find a means of reducing these demands. The difference between a demand and a simple request is plain to anyone.

The Seventh Step is where we make the change in our attitude which permits us, with humility as our guide, to move out from ourselves toward others and toward God. The whole emphasis of Step Seven is on humility. It is really saying to us that we now ought to be willing to try humility in seeking the removal of our other shortcomings just as we did when we admitted that we were powerless over alcohol, and came to believe that a Power greater than ourselves could restore us to sanity. If that degree of humility could enable us to find the grace by which such a deadly obsession could be banished, then there must be hope of the same result respecting any other problem we could possibly have.

Step Eight

"Made a list of all persons we had harmed, and became willing to make amends to them all."

STEPS Eight and Nine are concerned with personal relations. First, we take a look backward and try to discover where we have been at fault; next we make a vigorous attempt to repair the damage we have done; and third, having thus cleaned away the debris of the past, we consider how, with our newfound knowledge of ourselves, we may develop the best possible relations with every human being we know.

This is a very large order. It is a task which we may perform with increasing skill, but never really finish. Learning how to live in the greatest peace, partnership, and brotherhood with all men and women, of whatever description, is a moving and fascinating adventure. Every A.A. has found that he can make little headway in this new adventure of living until he first backtracks and really makes an accurate and unsparing survey of the human wreckage he has left in his wake. To a degree, he has already done this when taking moral inventory, but now the time has come when he ought to redouble his efforts to see how many people he has hurt, and in what ways. This reopening of emotional wounds, some old, some perhaps forgotten, and some still painfully festering, will at first look like a purposeless and pointless piece of surgery. But if a willing start is made,

then the great advantages of doing this will so quickly reveal themselves that the pain will be lessened as one obstacle after another melts away.

These obstacles, however, are very real. The first, and one
of the most difficult, has to do with forgiveness. The moment we ponder a twisted or broken relationship with another person, our emotions go on the defensive. To escape
looking at the wrongs we have done another, we resentfully
focus on the wrong he has done us. This is especially true if
he has, in fact, behaved badly at all. Triumphantly we seize
upon his misbehavior as the perfect excuse for minimizing
or forgetting our own.

Right here we need to fetch ourselves up sharply. It
doesn't make much sense when a real tosspot calls a kettle
black. Let's remember that alcoholics are not the only ones
bedeviled by sick emotions. Moreover, it is usually a fact
that our behavior when drinking has aggravated the defects
of others. We've repeatedly strained the patience of our
best friends to a snapping point, and have brought out the
very worst in those who didn't think much of us to begin
with. In many instances we are really dealing with fellow
sufferers, people whose woes we have increased. If we are
now about to ask forgiveness for ourselves, why shouldn't
we start out by forgiving them, one and all?

When listing the people we have harmed, most of us hit
another solid obstacle. We got a pretty severe shock when
we realized that we were preparing to make a face-to-face
admission of our wretched conduct to those we had hurt.
It had been embarrassing enough when in confidence we
had admitted these things to God, to ourselves, and to an-

other human being. But the prospect of actually visiting or even writing the people concerned now overwhelmed us, especially when we remembered in what poor favor we stood with most of them. There were cases, too, where we had damaged others who were still happily unaware of being hurt. Why, we cried, shouldn't bygones be bygones? Why do we have to think of these people at all? These were some of the ways in which fear conspired with pride to hinder our making a list of *all* the people we had harmed.

Some of us, though, tripped over a very different snag. We clung to the claim that when drinking we never hurt anybody but ourselves. Our families didn't suffer, because we always paid the bills and seldom drank at home. Our business associates didn't suffer, because we were usually on the job. Our reputations hadn't suffered, because we were certain few knew of our drinking. Those who did would sometimes assure us that, after all, a lively bender was only a good man's fault. What real harm, therefore, had we done? No more, surely, than we could easily mend with a few casual apologies.

This attitude, of course, is the end result of purposeful forgetting. It is an attitude which can only be changed by a deep and honest search of our motives and actions.

Though in some cases we cannot make restitution at all, and in some cases action ought to be deferred, we should nevertheless make an accurate and really exhaustive survey of our past life as it has affected other people. In many instances we shall find that though the harm done others has not been great, the emotional harm we have done ourselves has. Very deep, sometimes quite forgotten, damaging emotional conflicts persist below the level of consciousness. At the time of these occurrences, they may actually have given our emotions violent twists which have since discolored our personalities and altered our lives for the worse.

While the purpose of making restitution to others is paramount, it is equally necessary that we extricate from an examination of our personal relations every bit of information about ourselves and our fundamental difficulties that we can. Since defective relations with other human beings have nearly always been the immediate cause of our woes, including our alcoholism, no field of investigation could yield more satisfying and valuable rewards than this one. Calm, thoughtful reflection upon personal relations can deepen our insight. We can go far beyond those things which were superficially wrong with us, to see those flaws which were basic, flaws which sometimes were responsible for the whole pattern of our lives. Thoroughness, we have found, will pay—and pay handsomely.

We might next ask ourselves what we mean when we say that we have "harmed" other people. What kinds of "harm" do people do one another, anyway? To define the word "harm" in a practical way, we might call it the result of instincts in collision, which cause physical, mental, emotional, or spiritual damage to people. If our tempers are consistently bad, we arouse anger in others. If we lie or cheat, we deprive others not only of their worldly goods, but of their emotional security and peace of mind. We really issue them an invitation to become contemptuous and vengeful. If our sex conduct is selfish, we may excite jealousy, misery, and a strong desire to retaliate in kind.

Such gross misbehavior is not by any means a full cata-
logue of the harms we do. Let us think of some of the
subtler ones which can sometimes be quite as damaging.
Suppose that in our family lives we happen to be miserly,
irresponsible, callous, or cold. Suppose that we are irrita-
ble, critical, impatient, and humorless. Suppose we lavish
attention upon one member of the family and neglect the
others. What happens when we try to dominate the whole
family, either by a rule of iron or by a constant outpour-
ing of minute directions for just how their lives should be
lived from hour to hour? What happens when we wallow
in depression, self-pity oozing from every pore, and inflict
that upon those about us? Such a roster of harms done
others—the kind that make daily living with us as practicing alcoholics difficult and often unbearable—could be
extended almost indefinitely. When we take such personality traits as these into shop, office, and the society of our
fellows, they can do damage almost as extensive as that we
have caused at home.

Having carefully surveyed this whole area of human relations, and having decided exactly what personality traits
in us injured and disturbed others, we can now commence
to ransack memory for the people to whom we have given
offense. To put a finger on the nearby and most deeply
damaged ones shouldn't be hard to do. Then, as year by
year we walk back through our lives as far as memory will
reach, we shall be bound to construct a long list of people who have, to some extent or other, been affected. We
should, of course, ponder and weigh each instance carefully. We shall want to hold ourselves to the course of ad-

mitting the things *we* have done, meanwhile forgiving the wrongs done us, real or fancied. We should avoid extreme judgments, both of ourselves and of others involved. We must not exaggerate our defects or theirs. A quiet, objective view will be our steadfast aim.

Whenever our pencil falters, we can fortify and cheer ourselves by remembering what A.A. experience in this Step has meant to others. It is the beginning of the end of isolation from our fellows and from God.

Step Nine

"Made direct amends to such people wherever possible, except when to do so would injure them or others."

GOOD judgment, a careful sense of timing, courage, and prudence—these are the qualities we shall need when we take Step Nine.

After we have made the list of people we have harmed, have reflected carefully upon each instance, and have tried to possess ourselves of the right attitude in which to proceed, we will see that the making of direct amends divides those we should approach into several classes. There will be those who ought to be dealt with just as soon as we become reasonably confident that we can maintain our sobriety. There will be those to whom we can make only partial restitution, lest complete disclosures do them or others more harm than good. There will be other cases where action ought to be deferred, and still others in which by the very nature of the situation we shall never be able to make direct personal contact at all.

Most of us begin making certain kinds of direct amends from the day we join Alcoholics Anonymous. The moment we tell our families that we are really going to try the program, the process has begun. In this area there are seldom any questions of timing or caution. We want to come in the door shouting the good news. After coming from our first

meeting, or perhaps after we have finished reading the book
"Alcoholics Anonymous," we usually want to sit down with
some member of the family and readily admit the damage
we have done by our drinking. Almost always we want to
go further and admit other defects that have made us hard
to live with. This will be a very different occasion, and in
sharp contrast with those hangover mornings when we al-
ternated between reviling ourselves and blaming the family
(and everyone else) for our troubles. At this first sitting, it
is necessary only that we make a general admission of our
defects. It may be unwise at this stage to rehash certain harrowing episodes. Good judgment will suggest that we ought
to take our time. While we may be quite willing to reveal
the very worst, we must be sure to remember that we cannot
buy our own peace of mind at the expense of others.

    Much the same approach will apply at the office or fac-
tory. We shall at once think of a few people who know all
about our drinking, and who have been most affected by it.
But even in these cases, we may need to use a little more discretion than we did with the family. We may not want to say
anything for several weeks, or longer. First we will wish to
be reasonably certain that we are on the A.A. beam. Then
we are ready to go to these people, to tell them what A.A.
is, and what we are trying to do. Against this background
we can freely admit the damage we have done and make our
apologies. We can pay, or promise to pay, whatever obligations, financial or otherwise, we owe. The generous response
of most people to such quiet sincerity will often astonish us.
Even our severest and most justified critics will frequently
meet us more than halfway on the first trial.

This atmosphere of approval and praise is apt to be so exhilarating as to put us off balance by creating an insatiable appetite for more of the same. Or we may be tipped over in the other direction when, in rare cases, we get a cool and skeptical reception. This will tempt us to argue, or to press our point insistently. Or maybe it will tempt us to discouragement and pessimism. But if we have prepared ourselves well in advance, such reactions will not deflect us from our steady and even purpose.

After taking this preliminary trial at making amends, we may enjoy such a sense of relief that we conclude our task is finished. We will want to rest on our laurels. The temptation to skip the more humiliating and dreaded meetings that still remain may be great. We will often manufacture plausible excuses for dodging these issues entirely. Or we may just procrastinate, telling ourselves the time is not yet, when in reality we have already passed up many a fine chance to right a serious wrong. Let's not talk prudence while practicing evasion.

As soon as we begin to feel confident in our new way of life and have begun, by our behavior and example, to convince those about us that we are indeed changing for the better, it is usually safe to talk in complete frankness with those who have been seriously affected, even those who may be only a little or not at all aware of what we have done to them. The only exceptions we will make will be cases where our disclosure would cause actual harm. These conversations can begin in a casual or natural way. But if no such opportunity presents itself, at some point we will want to summon all our courage, head straight for the person concerned, and lay our cards on the table. We needn't wallow in excessive remorse before those we have harmed, but amends at this level should always be forthright and generous.

There can only be one consideration which should qualify our desire for a complete disclosure of the damage we have done. That will arise in the occasional situation where to make a full revelation would seriously harm the one to whom we are making amends. Or—quite as important—other people. We cannot, for example, unload a detailed account of extramarital adventuring upon the shoulders of our unsuspecting wife or husband. And even in those cases where such a matter must be discussed, let's try to avoid harming third parties, whoever they may be. It does not lighten our burden when we recklessly make the crosses of others heavier.

Many a razor-edged question can arise in other departments of life where this same principle is involved. Suppose, for instance, that we have drunk up a good chunk of our firm's money, whether by "borrowing" or on a heavily padded expense account. Suppose that this may continue to go undetected, if we say nothing. Do we instantly confess our irregularities to the firm, in the practical certainty that we will be fired and become unemployable? Are we going to be so rigidly righteous about making amends that we don't care what happens to the family and home? Or do we first consult those who are to be gravely affected? Do we lay the matter before our sponsor or spiritual adviser, earnestly asking God's help and guidance—meanwhile resolving to do the right thing when it becomes clear, cost what it may? Of course, there is no pat answer which can fit all such dilemmas. But all of them do require a complete willingness to make amends as fast and as far as may be possible in a given set of conditions.

Above all, we should try to be absolutely sure that we are not delaying because we are afraid. For the readiness to take the full consequences of our past acts, and to take responsibility for the well-being of others at the same time, is the very spirit of Step Nine.

Step Ten

"Continued to take personal inventory and when we were wrong promptly admitted it."

AS we work the first nine Steps, we prepare ourselves for the adventure of a new life. But when we approach Step Ten we commence to put our A.A. way of living to practical use, day by day, in fair weather or foul. Then comes the acid test: can we stay sober, keep in emotional balance, and live to good purpose under all conditions?

A continuous look at our assets and liabilities, and a real desire to learn and grow by this means, are necessities for us. We alcoholics have learned this the hard way. More experienced people, of course, in all times and places have practiced unsparing self-survey and criticism. For the wise have always known that no one can make much of his life until self-searching becomes a regular habit, until he is able to admit and accept what he finds, and until he patiently and persistently tries to correct what is wrong.

When a drunk has a terrific hangover because he drank heavily yesterday, he cannot live well today. But there is another kind of hangover which we all experience whether we are drinking or not. That is the emotional hangover, the direct result of yesterday's and sometimes today's excesses of negative emotion—anger, fear, jealousy, and the like. If we would live serenely today and tomorrow, we certainly need to eliminate these hangovers. This doesn't mean we need to wander morbidly around in the past. It requires an admission and correction of errors *now*. Our inventory enables us to settle with the past. When this is done, we are really able to leave it behind us. When our inventory is carefully taken, and we have made peace with ourselves, the conviction follows that tomorrow's challenges can be met as they come.

Although all inventories are alike in principle, the time factor does distinguish one from another. There's the spot-check inventory, taken at any time of the day, whenever we find ourselves getting tangled up. There's the one we take at day's end, when we review the happenings of the hours just past. Here we cast up a balance sheet, crediting ourselves with things well done, and chalking up debits where due. Then there are those occasions when alone, or in the company of our sponsor or spiritual adviser, we make a careful review of our progress since the last time. Many A.A.'s go in for annual or semiannual housecleanings. Many of us also like the experience of an occasional retreat from the outside world where we can quiet down for an undisturbed day or so of self-overhaul and meditation.

Aren't these practices joy-killers as well as time-consumers? Must A.A.'s spend most of their waking hours drearily rehashing their sins of omission or commission? Well, hardly. The emphasis on inventory is heavy only because a great many of us have never really acquired the habit of accurate self-appraisal. Once this healthy practice has become grooved, it will be so interesting and profitable that the time it takes won't be missed. For these minutes and sometimes hours spent in self-examination are bound to make all the other hours of our day better and happier. And at length our inventories become a regular part of everyday living, rather than something unusual or set apart.

Before we ask what a spot-check inventory is, let's look at the kind of setting in which such an inventory can do its work.

It is a spiritual axiom that every time we are disturbed, no matter what the cause, there is something wrong *with us*. If somebody hurts us and we are sore, we are in the wrong also. But are there no exceptions to this rule? What about "justifiable" anger? If somebody cheats us, aren't we entitled to be mad? Can't we be properly angry with self-righteous folk? For us of A.A. these are dangerous exceptions. We have found that justified anger ought to be left to those better qualified to handle it.

Few people have been more victimized by resentments than have we alcoholics. It mattered little whether our resentments were justified or not. A burst of temper could spoil a day, and a well-nursed grudge could make us miserably ineffective. Nor were we ever skillful in separating justified from unjustified anger. As we saw it, our wrath was always justified. Anger, that occasional luxury of more balanced people, could keep us on an emotional jag indefinitely. These emotional "dry benders" often led straight to the bottle. Other kinds of disturbances—jealousy, envy, self-pity, or hurt pride—did the same thing.

A spot-check inventory taken in the midst of such disturbances can be of very great help in quieting stormy emotions. Today's spot check finds its chief application to situations which arise in each day's march. The consideration of long-standing difficulties had better be postponed, when possible, to times deliberately set aside for that purpose. The quick inventory is aimed at our daily ups and downs, especially those where people or new events throw us off balance and tempt us to make mistakes.

In all these situations we need self-restraint, honest analysis of what is involved, a willingness to admit when the fault is ours, and an equal willingness to forgive when the fault is elsewhere. We need not be discouraged when we fall into the error of our old ways, for these disciplines are not easy. We shall look for progress, not for perfection.

Our first objective will be the development of self-restraint. This carries a top priority rating. When we speak or act hastily or rashly, the ability to be fair-minded and tolerant evaporates on the spot. One unkind tirade or one willful snap judgment can ruin our relation with another person for a whole day, or maybe a whole year. Nothing pays off like restraint of tongue and pen. We must avoid quick-tempered criticism and furious, power-driven argument. The same goes for sulking or silent scorn. These are emotional booby traps baited with pride and vengefulness. Our first job is to sidestep the traps. When we are tempted by the bait, we should train ourselves to step back and think. For we can neither think nor act to good purpose until the habit of self-restraint has become automatic.

Disagreeable or unexpected problems are not the only ones that call for self-control. We must be quite as careful when we begin to achieve some measure of importance and material success. For no people have ever loved personal triumphs more than we have loved them; we drank of success as of a wine which could never fail to make us feel elated. When temporary good fortune came our way, we indulged ourselves in fantasies of still greater victories over people and circumstances. Thus blinded by prideful self-confidence, we were apt to play the big shot. Of course, people turned away from us, bored or hurt.

Now that we're in A.A. and sober, and winning back the esteem of our friends and business associates, we find that we still need to exercise special vigilance. As an insurance against "big-shot-ism" we can often check ourselves by remembering that we are today sober only by the grace of God and that any success we may be having is far more His success than ours.

Finally, we begin to see that all people, including ourselves, are to some extent emotionally ill as well as frequently wrong, and then we approach true tolerance and see what real love for our fellows actually means. It will become more and more evident as we go forward that it is pointless to become angry, or to get hurt by people who, like us, are suffering from the pains of growing up.

Such a radical change in our outlook will take time, maybe a lot of time. Not many people can truthfully assert that they love everybody. Most of us must admit that we have loved but a few; that we have been quite indifferent to the many so long as none of them gave us trouble; and as for the remainder—well, we have really disliked or hated them. Although these attitudes are common enough, we A.A.'s find we need something much better in order to keep our balance. We can't stand it if we hate deeply. The idea that we can be possessively loving of a few, can ignore the many, and can continue to fear or hate *anybody*, has to be abandoned, if only a little at a time.

We can try to stop making unreasonable demands upon those we love. We can show kindness where we had shown none. With those we dislike we can begin to practice justice and courtesy, perhaps going out of our way to understand and help them.

Whenever we fail any of these people, we can promptly admit it—to ourselves always, and to them also, when the admission would be helpful. Courtesy, kindness, justice, and love are the keynotes by which we may come into harmony with practically anybody. When in doubt we can always pause, saying, "Not my will, but Thine, be done." And we can often ask ourselves, "Am I doing to others as I would have them do to me—today?"

When evening comes, perhaps just before going to sleep, many of us draw up a balance sheet for the day. This is a good place to remember that inventory-taking is not always done in red ink. It's a poor day indeed when we haven't done *something* right. As a matter of fact, the waking hours are usually well filled with things that are constructive. Good intentions, good thoughts, and good acts are there for us to see. Even when we have tried hard and failed, we may chalk that up as one of the greatest credits of all. Under these conditions, the pains of failure are converted into assets. Out of them we receive the stimulation we need to go forward. Someone who knew what he was talking about once remarked that pain was the touchstone of all spiritual progress. How heartily we A.A.'s can agree with him, for we know that the pains of drinking had to come before sobriety, and emotional turmoil before serenity.

As we glance down the debit side of the day's ledger, we should carefully examine our motives in each thought or act that appears to be wrong. In most cases our motives won't be hard to see and understand. When prideful, angry, jealous, anxious, or fearful, we acted accordingly, and that was that. Here we need only recognize that we did act or think badly, try to visualize how we might have done better, and resolve with God's help to carry these lessons over into tomorrow, making, of course, any amends still neglected.

But in other instances only the closest scrutiny will reveal what our true motives were. There are cases where our ancient enemy, rationalization, has stepped in and has justified conduct which was really wrong. The temptation here is to imagine that we had good motives and reasons when we really didn't.

We "constructively criticized" someone who needed it, when our real motive was to win a useless argument. Or, the person concerned not being present, we thought we were helping others to understand him, when in actuality our true motive was to feel superior by pulling him down. We sometimes hurt those we love because they need to be "taught a lesson," when we really want to punish. We were depressed and complained we felt bad, when in fact we were mainly asking for sympathy and attention. This odd trait of mind and emotion, this perverse wish to hide a bad motive underneath a good one, permeates human affairs from top to bottom. This subtle and elusive kind of self-righteousness can underlie the smallest act or thought.

Learning daily to spot, admit, and correct these flaws is the essence of character-building and good living. An honest regret for harms done, a genuine gratitude for blessings received, and a willingness to try for better things tomorrow will be the permanent assets we shall seek.

Having so considered our day, not omitting to take due note of things well done, and having searched our hearts with neither fear nor favor, we can truly thank God for the blessings we have received and sleep in good conscience.

Step Eleven

"Sought through prayer and meditation to im-
prove our conscious contact with God <u>as we un-</u>
<u>derstood Him</u>, praying only for knowledge of
His will for us and the power to carry that out."

PRAYER and meditation are our principal means of conscious contact with God.

We A.A.'s are active folk, enjoying the satisfactions of
dealing with the realities of life, usually for the first time in
our lives, and strenuously trying to help the next alcoholic
who comes along. So it isn't surprising that we often tend
to slight serious meditation and prayer as something not
really necessary. To be sure, we feel it is something that
might help us to meet an occasional emergency, but at first
many of us are apt to regard it as a somewhat mysterious skill of clergymen, from which we may hope to get a
secondhand benefit. Or perhaps we don't believe in these
things at all.

To certain newcomers and to those one-time agnostics
who still cling to the A.A. group as their higher power,
claims for the power of prayer may, despite all the logic
and experience in proof of it, still be unconvincing or quite
objectionable. Those of us who once felt this way can certainly understand and sympathize. We well remember how
something deep inside us kept rebelling against the idea of
bowing before any God. Many of us had strong logic, too,

which "proved" there was no God whatever. What about all the accidents, sickness, cruelty, and injustice in the world? What about all those unhappy lives which were the direct result of unfortunate birth and uncontrollable circumstances? Surely there could be no justice in this scheme of things, and therefore no God at all.

Sometimes we took a slightly different tack. Sure, we said to ourselves, the hen probably did come before the egg. No doubt the universe had a "first cause" of some sort, the God of the Atom, maybe, hot and cold by turns. But certainly there wasn't any evidence of a God who knew or cared about human beings. We liked A.A. all right, and were quick to say that it had done miracles. But we recoiled from meditation and prayer as obstinately as the scientist who refused to perform a certain experiment lest it prove his pet theory wrong. Of course we finally did experiment, and when unexpected results followed, we felt different; in fact we *knew* different; and so we were sold on meditation and prayer. And that, we have found, can happen to anybody who tries. It has been well said that "almost the only scoffers at prayer are those who never tried it enough."

Those of us who have come to make regular use of prayer would no more do without it than we would refuse air, food, or sunshine. And for the same reason. When we refuse air, light, or food, the body suffers. And when we turn away from meditation and prayer, we likewise deprive our minds, our emotions, and our intuitions of vitally needed support. As the body can fail its purpose for lack of nourishment, so can the soul. We all need the light of

God's reality, the nourishment of His strength, and the atmosphere of His grace. To an amazing extent the facts of A.A. life confirm this ageless truth.

There is a direct linkage among self-examination, meditation, and prayer. Taken separately, these practices can bring much relief and benefit. But when they are logically related and interwoven, the result is an unshakable foundation for life. Now and then we may be granted a glimpse of that ultimate reality which is God's kingdom. And we will be comforted and assured that our own destiny in that realm will be secure for so long as we try, however falteringly, to find and do the will of our own Creator.

As we have seen, self-searching is the means by which we bring new vision, action, and grace to bear upon the dark and negative side of our natures. It is a step in the development of that kind of humility that makes it possible for us to receive God's help. Yet it is only a step. We will want to go further.

We will want the good that is in us all, even in the worst of us, to flower and to grow. Most certainly we shall need bracing air and an abundance of food. But first of all we shall want sunlight; nothing much can grow in the dark. Meditation is our step out into the sun. How, then, shall we meditate?

The actual experience of meditation and prayer across the centuries is, of course, immense. The world's libraries and places of worship are a treasure trove for all seekers. It is to be hoped that every A.A. who has a religious connection which emphasizes meditation will return to the practice of that devotion as never before. But what about the rest of us who, less fortunate, don't even know how to begin?

Well, we might start like this. First let's look at a really good prayer. We won't have far to seek; the great men and women of all religions have left us a wonderful supply. Here let us consider one that is a classic.

Its author was a man who for several hundred years now has been rated as a saint. We won't be biased or scared off by that fact, because although he was not an alcoholic he did, like us, go through the emotional wringer. And as he came out the other side of that painful experience, this prayer was his expression of what he could then see, feel, and wish to become:

"Lord, make me a channel of thy peace—that where there is hatred, I may bring love—that where there is wrong, I may bring the spirit of forgiveness—that where there is discord, I may bring harmony—that where there is error, I may bring truth—that where there is doubt, I may bring faith—that where there is despair, I may bring hope—that where there are shadows, I may bring light— that where there is sadness, I may bring joy. Lord, grant that I may seek rather to comfort than to be comforted— to understand, than to be understood—to love, than to be loved. For it is by self-forgetting that one finds. It is by for-giving that one is forgiven. It is by dying that one awakens to Eternal Life. Amen."

As beginners in meditation, we might now reread this prayer several times very slowly, savoring every word and trying to take in the deep meaning of each phrase and idea. It will help if we can drop all resistance to what our friend says. For in meditation, debate has no place. We rest quietly with the thoughts of someone who knows, so that we may experience and learn.

As though lying upon a sunlit beach, let us relax and breathe deeply of the spiritual atmosphere with which the grace of this prayer surrounds us. Let us become willing to partake and be strengthened and lifted up by the sheer spiritual power, beauty, and love of which these magnificent words are the carriers. Let us look now upon the sea and ponder what its mystery is; and let us lift our eyes to the far horizon, beyond which we shall seek all those wonders still unseen.

"Shucks!" says somebody. "This is nonsense. It isn't practical."

When such thoughts break in, we might recall, a little ruefully, how much store we used to set by imagination as it tried to create reality out of bottles. Yes, we reveled in that sort of thinking, didn't we? And though sober nowadays, don't we often try to do much the same thing? Perhaps our trouble was not that we used our imagination. Perhaps the real trouble was our almost total inability to point imagination toward the right objectives. There's nothing the matter with *constructive* imagination; all sound achievement rests upon it. After all, no man can build a house until he first envisions a plan for it. Well, meditation is like that, too; it helps to envision our spiritual objective before we try to move toward it. So let's get back to that sunlit beach—or to the plains or to the mountains, if you prefer.

When, by such simple devices, we have placed ourselves

in a mood in which we can focus undisturbed on constructive imagination, we might proceed like this:

Once more we read our prayer, and again try to see what
its inner essence is. We'll think now about the man who
first uttered the prayer. First of all, he wanted to become a
"channel." Then he asked for the grace to bring love, forgiveness, harmony, truth, faith, hope, light, and joy to every human being he could.

Next came the expression of an aspiration and a hope
for himself. He hoped, God willing, that he might be able to
find some of these treasures, too. This he would try to do by
what he called self-forgetting. What did he mean by "self-
forgetting," and how did he propose to accomplish that?

He thought it better to give comfort than to receive it;
better to understand than to be understood; better to forgive than to be forgiven.

This much could be a fragment of what is called meditation, perhaps our very first attempt at a mood, a flier into
the realm of spirit, if you like. It ought to be followed by
a good look at where we stand now, and a further look
at what might happen in our lives were we able to move
closer to the ideal we have been trying to glimpse. Meditation is something which can always be further developed.
It has no boundaries, either of width or height. Aided by
such instruction and example as we can find, it is essen-
tially an individual adventure, something which each one
of us works out in his own way. But its object is always the
same: to improve our conscious contact with God, with
His grace, wisdom, and love. And let's always remember
that meditation is in reality intensely practical. One of its

first fruits is emotional balance. With it we can broaden and deepen the channel between ourselves and God as we understand Him.

Now, what of prayer? Prayer is the raising of the heart and mind to God—and in this sense it includes meditation. How may we go about it? And how does it fit in with meditation? Prayer, as commonly understood, is a petition to God. Having opened our channel as best we can, we try to ask for those right things of which we and others are in the greatest need. And we think that the whole range of our needs is well defined by that part of Step Eleven which says: "…knowledge of His will for us and the power to carry that out." A request for this fits in any part of our day.

In the morning we think of the hours to come. Perhaps we think of our day's work and the chances it may afford us to be useful and helpful, or of some special problem that it may bring. Possibly today will see a continuation of a serious and as yet unresolved problem left over from yesterday. Our immediate temptation will be to ask for specific solutions to specific problems, and for the ability to help other people as we have already thought they should be helped. In that case, we are asking God to do it *our* way. Therefore, we ought to consider each request carefully to see what its real merit is. Even so, when making specific requests, it will be well to add to each one of them this qualification: "…if it be Thy will." We ask simply that throughout the day God place in us the best understanding of His will that we can have for that day, and that we be given the grace by which we may carry it out.

As the day goes on, we can pause where situations must

be met and decisions made, and renew the simple request: "Thy will, not mine, be done." If at these points our emotional disturbance happens to be great, we will more surely keep our balance, provided we remember, and repeat to ourselves, a particular prayer or phrase that has appealed to us in our reading or meditation. Just saying it over and over will often enable us to clear a channel choked up with anger, fear, frustration, or misunderstanding, and permit us to return to the surest help of all—our search for God's will, not our own, in the moment of stress. At these critical moments, if we remind ourselves that "it is better to comfort than to be comforted, to understand than to be understood, to love than to be loved," we will be following the intent of Step Eleven.

Of course, it is reasonable and understandable that the question is often asked: "*Why* can't we take a specific and troubling dilemma straight to God, and in prayer secure from Him sure and definite answers to our requests?"

This can be done, but it has hazards. We have seen A.A.'s ask with much earnestness and faith for God's explicit guidance on matters ranging all the way from a shattering domestic or financial crisis to correcting a minor personal fault, like tardiness. Quite often, however, the thoughts that *seem* to come from God are not answers at all. They prove to be well-intentioned unconscious rationalizations. The A.A., or indeed any man, who tries to run his life rigidly by this kind of prayer, by this self-serving demand of God for replies, is a particularly disconcerting individual. To any questioning or criticism of his actions he instantly proffers his reliance upon prayer for guidance in all matters great or small. He may have forgotten the possibility that his own wishful thinking and the human tendency to rationalize have distorted his so-called guidance. With the best of intentions, he tends to force his own will into all sorts of situations and problems with the comfortable assurance that he is acting under God's specific direction. Under such an illusion, he can of course create great havoc without in the least intending it.

We also fall into another similar temptation. We form ideas as to what we think God's will is for other people. We say to ourselves, "This one ought to be cured of his fatal malady," or "That one ought to be relieved of his emotional pain," and we pray for these specific things. Such prayers, of course, are fundamentally good acts, but often they are based upon a supposition that we know God's will for the person for whom we pray. This means that side by side with an earnest prayer there can be a certain amount of presumption and conceit in us. It is A.A.'s experience that particularly in these cases we ought to pray that God's will, whatever it is, be done for others as well as for ourselves.

In A.A. we have found that the actual good results of prayer are beyond question. They are matters of knowledge and experience. All those who have persisted have found strength not ordinarily their own. They have found wisdom beyond their usual capability. And they have increasingly found a peace of mind which can stand firm in the face of difficult circumstances.

We discover that we do receive guidance for our lives to just about the extent that we stop making demands upon God to give it to us on order and on our terms. Almost any experienced A.A. will tell how his affairs have taken remarkable and unexpected turns for the better as he tried to improve his conscious contact with God. He will also report that out of every season of grief or suffering, when the hand of God seemed heavy or even unjust, new lessons for living were learned, new resources of courage were uncovered, and that finally, inescapably, the conviction came that God *does* "move in a mysterious way His wonders to perform."

All this should be very encouraging news for those who recoil from prayer because they don't believe in it, or because they feel themselves cut off from God's help and direction. All of us, without exception, pass through times when we can pray only with the greatest exertion of will. Occasionally we go even further than this. We are seized with a rebellion so sickening that we simply won't pray. When these things happen we should not think too ill of ourselves. We should simply resume prayer as soon as we can, doing what we know to be good for us.

Perhaps one of the greatest rewards of meditation and prayer is the sense of *belonging* that comes to us. We no longer live in a completely hostile world. We are no longer lost and frightened and purposeless. The moment we catch even a glimpse of God's will, the moment we begin to see truth, justice, and love as the real and eternal things in life, we are no longer deeply disturbed by all the seeming evidence to the contrary that surrounds us in purely human affairs. We know that God lovingly watches over us. We know that when we turn to Him, all will be well with us, here and hereafter.

Step Twelve

"Having had a spiritual awakening as the result of these steps, we tried to carry this message to alcoholics, and to practice these principles in all our affairs."

THE joy of living is the theme of A.A.'s Twelfth Step, and action is its key word. Here we turn outward toward our fellow alcoholics who are still in distress. Here we experience the kind of giving that asks no rewards. Here we begin to practice all Twelve Steps of the program in our daily lives so that we and those about us may find emotional sobriety. When the Twelfth Step is seen in its full implication, it is really talking about the kind of love that has no price tag on it.

Our Twelfth Step also says that as a result of practicing all the Steps, we have each found something called a spiritual awakening. To new A.A.'s, this often seems like a very dubious and improbable state of affairs. "What do you mean when you talk about a 'spiritual awakening'?" they ask.

Maybe there are as many definitions of spiritual awakening as there are people who have had them. But certainly each genuine one has something in common with all the others. And these things which they have in common are not too hard to understand. When a man or a woman has a spiritual awakening, the most important meaning of it is that he has now become able to do, feel, and believe that which he could not do before on his unaided strength and resources alone. He has been granted a gift which amounts to a new state of consciousness and being. He has been set on a path which tells him he is really going somewhere, that life is not a dead end, not something to be endured or mastered. In a very real sense he has been transformed, because he has laid hold of a source of strength which, in one way or another, he had hitherto denied himself. He finds himself in possession of a degree of honesty, tolerance, unselfishness, peace of mind, and love of which he had thought himself quite incapable. What he has received is a free gift, and yet usually, at least in some small part, he has made himself ready to receive it.

A.A.'s manner of making ready to receive this gift lies in the practice of the Twelve Steps in our program. So let's consider briefly what we have been trying to do up to this point:

Step One showed us an amazing paradox: We found that we were totally unable to be rid of the alcohol obsession until we first admitted that we were powerless over it. In Step Two we saw that since we could not restore ourselves to sanity, some Higher Power must necessarily do so if we were to survive. Consequently, in Step Three we turned our will and our lives over to the care of God as we understood Him. For the time being, we who were atheist or agnostic discovered that our own group, or A.A. as a whole, would suffice as a higher power. Beginning with Step Four, we commenced to search out the things in ourselves which had brought us to physical, moral, and spiritual bankruptcy. We made a searching and fearless moral inventory. Looking at Step Five, we decided that an inventory, taken alone, wouldn't be enough. We knew we would have to quit the deadly business of living alone with our conflicts, and in honesty confide these to God and another human being. At Step Six, many of us balked—for the practical reason that we did not wish to have all our defects of character removed, because we still loved some of them too much. Yet we knew we had to make a settlement with the fundamental principle of Step Six. So we decided that while we still had some flaws of character that we could not yet relinquish, we ought nevertheless to quit our stubborn, rebellious hanging on to them. We said to ourselves, "This I cannot do today, perhaps, but I can stop crying out 'No, never!'" Then, in Step Seven, we humbly asked God to remove our shortcomings such as He could or would under the conditions of the day we asked. In Step Eight, we continued our house-cleaning, for we saw that we were not only in conflict with ourselves, but also with people and situations in the world in which we lived. We had to begin to make our peace, and so we listed the people we had harmed and became willing to set things right. We followed this up in Step Nine by making direct amends to those concerned, except when it would injure them or other people. By this time, at Step Ten, we had begun to get a basis for daily living, and we keenly realized that we would need to continue taking personal inventory, and that when we were in the wrong we ought to admit it promptly. In Step Eleven we saw that if a Higher Power had restored us to sanity and had enabled us to live with some peace of mind in a sorely troubled world, then such a Higher Power was worth knowing better, by as direct contact as possible. The persistent use of meditation and prayer, we found, did open the channel so that where there had been a trickle, there now was a river which led to sure power and safe guidance from God as we were increasingly better able to understand Him.

So, practicing these Steps, we had a spiritual awakening about which finally there was no question. Looking at those who were only beginning and still doubted themselves, the rest of us were able to see the change setting in. From great numbers of such experiences, we could predict that the doubter who still claimed that he hadn't got the "spiritual angle," and who still considered his well-loved A.A. group the higher power, would presently love God and call Him by name.

Now, what about the rest of the Twelfth Step? The wonderful energy it releases and the eager action by which it carries our message to the next suffering alcoholic and which finally translates the Twelve Steps into action upon all our affairs is the payoff, the magnificent reality, of Alcoholics Anonymous.

Even the newest of newcomers finds undreamed rewards as he tries to help his brother alcoholic, the one who is even blinder than he. This is indeed the kind of giving that actually demands nothing. He does not expect his brother sufferer to pay him, or even to love him. And then he discovers that by the divine paradox of this kind of giving he has found his own reward, whether his brother has yet received anything or not. His own character may still be gravely defective, but he somehow knows that God has enabled him to make a mighty beginning, and he senses that he stands at the edge of new mysteries, joys, and experiences of which he had never even dreamed.

Practically every A.A. member declares that no satisfaction has been deeper and no joy greater than in a Twelfth Step job well done. To watch the eyes of men and women open with wonder as they move from darkness into light, to see their lives quickly fill with new purpose and meaning, to see whole families reassembled, to see the alcoholic outcast received back into his community in full citizenship, and above all to watch these people awaken to the presence of a loving God in their lives—these things are the substance of what we receive as we carry A.A.'s message to the next alcoholic.

Nor is this the only kind of Twelfth Step work. We sit in A.A. meetings and listen, not only to receive something ourselves, but to give the reassurance and support which our presence can bring. If our turn comes to speak at a meeting, we again try to carry A.A.'s message. Whether our audience is one or many, it is still Twelfth Step work. There are many opportunities even for those of us who feel unable to speak at meetings or who are so situated that we cannot do much face-to-face Twelfth Step work. We can be the ones who take on the unspectacular but important tasks that make good Twelfth Step work possible, perhaps arranging for the coffee and cake after the meetings, where so many skeptical, suspicious newcomers have found confidence and comfort in the laughter and talk. This is Twelfth Step work in the very best sense of the word. "Freely ye have received; freely give…" is the core of this part of Step Twelve.

We may often pass through Twelfth Step experiences where we will seem to be temporarily off the beam. These will appear as big setbacks at the time, but will be seen later as stepping-stones to better things. For example, we may set our hearts on getting a particular person sobered up, and after doing all we can for months, we see him relapse. Perhaps this will happen in a succession of cases, and we may be deeply discouraged as to our ability to carry A.A.'s message. Or we may encounter the reverse situation, in which we are highly elated because we seem to have been successful. Here the temptation is to become rather possessive of these newcomers. Perhaps we try to give them advice about their affairs which we aren't really competent to give or ought not give at all. Then we are hurt and confused when the advice is rejected, or when it is accepted and brings still greater confusion. By a great deal of ardent Twelfth Step work we sometimes carry the message to so many alcoholics that they place us in a position of trust. They make us, let us say, the group's chairman. Here again we are presented with the temptation to overmanage things, and sometimes this results in rebuffs and other consequences which are hard to take.

But in the longer run we clearly realize that these are only the pains of growing up, and nothing but good can come from them if we turn more and more to the entire Twelve Steps for the answers.

Now comes the biggest question yet. What about the practice of these principles in *all* our affairs? Can we love the whole pattern of living as eagerly as we do the small segment of it we discover when we try to help other alcoholics achieve sobriety? Can we bring the same spirit of love and tolerance into our sometimes deranged family lives that we bring to our A.A. group? Can we have the same kind of confidence and faith in these people who have been infected and sometimes crippled by our own illness that we have in our sponsors? Can we actually carry the A.A. spirit into our daily work? Can we meet our newly recognized responsibilities to the world at large? And can we bring new purpose and devotion to the religion of our choice? Can we find a new joy of living in trying to do something about all these things?

Furthermore, how shall we come to terms with seeming failure or success? Can we now accept and adjust to either without despair or pride? Can we accept poverty, sickness, loneliness, and bereavement with courage and serenity? Can we steadfastly content ourselves with the humbler, yet sometimes more durable, satisfactions when the brighter, more glittering achievements are denied us?

The A.A. answer to these questions about living is "Yes, all of these things are possible." We know this because we see monotony, pain, and even calamity turned to good use by those who keep on trying to practice A.A.'s Twelve Steps. And if these are facts of life for the many alcoholics who have recovered in A.A., they can become the facts of life for many more.

Of course all A.A.'s, even the best, fall far short of such achievements as a consistent thing. Without necessarily taking that first drink, we often get quite far off the beam. Our troubles sometimes begin with indifference. We are sober and happy in our A.A. work. Things go well at home and office. We naturally congratulate ourselves on what later proves to be a far too easy and superficial point of view. We temporarily cease to grow because we feel satisfied that there is no need for *all* of A.A.'s Twelve Steps for us. We are doing fine on a few of them. Maybe we are doing fine on only two of them, the First Step and that part of the Twelfth where we "carry the message." In A.A. slang, that blissful state is known as "two-stepping." And it can go on for years.

The best-intentioned of us can fall for the "two-step" illusion. Sooner or later the pink cloud stage wears off and things go disappointingly dull. We begin to think that A.A. doesn't pay off after all. We become puzzled and discouraged.

Then perhaps life, as it has a way of doing, suddenly hands us a great big lump that we can't begin to swallow, let alone digest. We fail to get a worked-for promotion. We lose that good job. Maybe there are serious domestic or romantic difficulties, or perhaps that boy we thought God was looking after becomes a military casualty.

What then? Have we alcoholics in A.A. got, or can we get, the resources to meet these calamities which come to so many? These were problems of life which we could never face up to. Can we now, with the help of God as we understand Him, handle them as well and as bravely as our nonalcoholic friends often do? Can we transform these calamities into assets, sources of growth and comfort to ourselves and those about us? Well, we surely have a chance if we switch from "two-stepping" to "twelve-stepping," if we are willing to receive that grace of God which can sustain and strengthen us in any catastrophe.

Our basic troubles are the same as everyone else's, but when an honest effort is made "to practice these principles in all our affairs," well-grounded A.A.'s seem to have the ability, by God's grace, to take these troubles in stride and turn them into demonstrations of faith. We have seen A.A.'s suffer lingering and fatal illness with little complaint, and often in good cheer. We have sometimes seen families broken apart by misunderstanding, tensions, or actual infidelity, who are reunited by the A.A. way of life.

Though the earning power of most A.A.'s is relatively high, we have some members who never seem to get on their feet moneywise, and still others who encounter heavy financial reverses. Ordinarily we see these situations met with fortitude and faith.

Like most people, we have found that we can take our big lumps as they come. But also like others, we often discover a greater challenge in the lesser and more continuous problems of life. Our answer is in still more spiritual development. Only by this means can we improve our chances for really happy and useful living. And as we grow spiritually, we find that our old attitudes toward our instincts need to undergo drastic revisions. Our desires for emotional security and wealth, for personal prestige and power, for romance, and for family satisfactions—all these have to be tempered and redirected. We have learned that the satisfaction of instincts cannot be the sole end and aim of our lives. If we place instincts first, we have got the cart before the horse; we shall be pulled backward into disillusionment. But when we are willing to place spiritual growth first—then and only then do we have a real chance.

After we come into A.A., if we go on growing, our attitudes and actions toward security—emotional security and financial security—commence to change profoundly. Our demand for emotional security, for our own way, had constantly thrown us into unworkable relations with other people. Though we were sometimes quite unconscious of this, the result always had been the same. Either we had tried to play God and dominate those about us, or we had insisted on being overdependent upon them. Where people had temporarily let us run their lives as though they were still children, we had felt very happy and secure ourselves. But when they finally resisted or ran away, we were bitterly hurt and disappointed. We blamed them, being quite unable to see that our unreasonable demands had been the cause.

When we had taken the opposite tack and had insisted, like infants ourselves, that people protect and take care of us or that the world owed us a living, then the result had been equally unfortunate. This often caused the people we had loved most to push us aside or perhaps desert us entirely. Our disillusionment had been hard to bear. We couldn't imagine people acting that way toward us. We had failed to see that though adult in years we were still behaving childishly, trying to turn everybody—friends, wives, husbands, even the world itself—into protective parents. We had refused to learn the very hard lesson that overdependence upon people is unsuccessful because all people are fallible, and even the best of them will sometimes let us down, especially when our demands for attention become unreasonable.

As we made spiritual progress, we saw through these fallacies. It became clear that if we ever were to feel emotionally secure among grown-up people, we would have to put our lives on a give-and-take basis; we would have to develop the sense of being in partnership or brotherhood with all those around us. We saw that we would need to give constantly of ourselves without demands for repayment. When we persistently did this we gradually found that people were attracted to us as never before. And even if they failed us, we could be understanding and not too seriously affected.

When we developed still more, we discovered the best possible source of emotional stability to be God Himself. We found that dependence upon His perfect justice, forgiveness, and love was healthy, and that it would work where nothing else would. If we really depended upon God, we couldn't very well play God to our fellows nor would we feel the urge wholly to rely on human protection and care. These were the new attitudes that finally brought many of us an inner strength and peace that could not be deeply shaken by the shortcomings of others or by any calamity not of our own making.

This new outlook was, we learned, something especially necessary to us alcoholics. For alcoholism had been a lonely business, even though we had been surrounded by people who loved us. But when self-will had driven everybody away and our isolation had become complete, it caused us to play the big shot in cheap barrooms and then fare forth alone on the street to depend upon the charity of passersby. We were still trying to find emotional security by being dominating or dependent upon others. Even when our fortunes had not ebbed that much and we nevertheless found ourselves alone in the world, we still vainly tried to be secure by some unhealthy kind of domination or dependence. For those of us who were like that, A.A. had a very special meaning. Through it we begin to learn right relations with people who understand us; we don't have to be alone any more.

Most married folks in A.A. have very happy homes. To a surprising extent, A.A. has offset the damage to family life brought about by years of alcoholism. But just like all other societies, we do have sex and marital problems, and sometimes they are distressingly acute. Permanent marriage breakups and separations, however, are unusual in A.A. Our main problem is not how we are to stay married; it is how to be more happily married by eliminating the severe emotional twists that have so often stemmed from alcoholism.

Nearly every sound human being experiences, at some time in life, a compelling desire to find a mate of the opposite sex with whom the fullest possible union can be made —spiritual, mental, emotional, and physical. This mighty urge is the root of great human accomplishments, a creative energy that deeply influences our lives. God fashioned us that way. So our question will be this: How, by ignorance, compulsion, and self-will, do we misuse this gift for our own destruction? We A.A.'s cannot pretend to offer full answers to age-old perplexities, but our own experience does provide certain answers that work for us.

When alcoholism strikes, very unnatural situations may

develop which work against marriage partnership and compatible union. If the man is affected, the wife must become the head of the house, often the breadwinner. As matters get worse, the husband becomes a sick and irresponsible child who needs to be looked after and extricated from endless scrapes and impasses. Very gradually, and usually without any realization of the fact, the wife is forced to become the mother of an erring boy. And if she had a strong maternal instinct to begin with, the situation is aggravated. Obviously not much partnership can exist under these conditions. The wife usually goes on doing the best she knows how, but meanwhile the alcoholic alternately loves and hates her maternal care. A pattern is thereby established that may take a lot of undoing later on. Nevertheless, under the influence of A.A.'s Twelve Steps, these situations are often set right.[*]

When the distortion has been great, however, a long period of patient striving may be necessary. After the husband joins A.A., the wife may become discontented, even highly resentful that Alcoholics Anonymous has done the very thing that all her years of devotion had failed to do. Her husband may become so wrapped up in A.A. and his new friends that he is inconsiderately away from home more than when he drank. Seeing her unhappiness, he recommends A.A.'s Twelve Steps and tries to teach her how to live. She naturally feels that for years she has made a far better job of living than he has.

---

[*] In adapted form, the Steps are also used by Al-Anon Family Groups. Not a part of A.A., this worldwide fellowship consists of spouses and other relatives or friends of alcoholics (in A.A. or still drinking). Its headquarters address is 1600 Corporate Landing Pkwy., Virginia Beach, VA 23454-5617. Website: www.al-anon.org,

Both of them blame each other and ask when their marriage is ever going to be happy again. They may even begin to suspect it had never been any good in the first place.

Compatibility, of course, can be so impossibly damaged that a separation may be necessary. But those cases are the unusual ones. The alcoholic, realizing what his wife has endured, and now fully understanding how much he himself did to damage her and his children, nearly always takes up his marriage responsibilities with a willingness to repair what he can and to accept what he can't. He persistently tries all of A.A.'s Twelve Steps in his home, often with fine results. At this point he firmly but lovingly commences to behave like a partner instead of like a bad boy. And above all he is finally convinced that reckless romancing is not a way of life for him.

A.A. has many single alcoholics who wish to marry and are in a position to do so. Some marry fellow A.A.'s. How do they come out? On the whole these marriages are very good ones. Their common suffering as drinkers, their common interest in A.A. and spiritual things, often enhance such unions. It is only where "boy meets girl on A.A. campus," and love follows at first sight, that difficulties may develop. The prospective partners need to be solid A.A.'s and long enough acquainted to know that their compatibility at spiritual, mental, and emotional levels is a fact and not wishful thinking. They need to be as sure as possible that no deep-lying emotional handicap in either will be likely to rise up under later pressures to cripple them. The considerations are equally true and important for the A.A.'s who marry "outside" A.A. With clear understanding and right, grown-up attitudes, very happy results do follow.

And what can be said of many A.A. members who, for a variety of reasons, cannot have a family life? At first many of these feel lonely, hurt, and left out as they witness so much domestic happiness about them. If they cannot have this kind of happiness, can A.A. offer them satisfactions of similar worth and durability? Yes—whenever they try hard to seek them out. Surrounded by so many A.A. friends, these so-called loners tell us they no longer feel alone. In partnership with others—women and men—they can devote themselves to any number of ideas, people, and constructive projects. Free of marital responsibilities, they can participate in enterprises which would be denied to family men and women. We daily see such members render prodigies of service, and receive great joys in return.

Where the possession of money and material things was concerned, our outlook underwent the same revolutionary change. With a few exceptions, all of us had been spend-thrifts. We threw money about in every direction with the purpose of pleasing ourselves and impressing other people. In our drinking time, we acted as if the money supply was inexhaustible, though between binges we'd sometimes go to the other extreme and become almost miserly. Without realizing it we were just accumulating funds for the next spree. Money was the symbol of pleasure and self-importance. When our drinking had become much worse, money was only an urgent requirement which could supply us with the next drink and the temporary comfort of oblivion it brought.

Upon entering A.A., these attitudes were sharply reversed, often going much too far in the opposite direction. The spectacle of years of waste threw us into panic. There simply wouldn't be time, we thought, to rebuild our shattered fortunes. How could we ever take care of those awful debts, possess a decent home, educate the kids, and set something by for old age? Financial importance was no longer our principal aim; we now clamored for material security. Even when we were well reestablished in our business, these terrible fears often continued to haunt us. This made us misers and penny pinchers all over again. Complete financial security we must have—or else. We forgot that most alcoholics in A.A. have an earning power considerably above average; we forgot the immense goodwill of our brother A.A.'s who were only too eager to help us to better jobs when we deserved them; we forgot the actual or potential financial insecurity of every human being in the world. And, worst of all, we forgot God. In money matters we had faith only in ourselves, and not too much of that.

This all meant, of course, that we were still far off balance. When a job still looked like a mere means of getting money rather than an opportunity for service, when the acquisition of money for financial independence looked more important than a right dependence upon God, we were still the victims of unreasonable fears. And these were fears which would make a serene and useful existence, at any financial level, quite impossible.

But as time passed we found that with the help of A.A.'s Twelve Steps we could lose those fears, no matter what our material prospects were. We could cheerfully perform humble labor without worrying about tomorrow. If our circumstances happened to be good, we no longer dreaded a change for the worse, for we had learned that these troubles could be turned into great values. It did not matter too much what our material condition was, but it did matter what our spiritual condition was. Money gradually became our servant and not our master. It became a means of exchanging love and service with those about us. When, with God's help, we calmly accepted our lot, then we found we could live at peace with ourselves and show others who still suffered the same fears that they could get over them, too. We found that freedom from fear was more important than freedom from want.

Let's here take note of our improved outlook upon the problems of personal importance, power, ambition, and leadership. These were reefs upon which many of us came to shipwreck during our drinking careers.

Practically every boy in the United States dreams of becoming our President. He wants to be his country's number one man. As he gets older and sees the impossibility of this, he can smile good-naturedly at his childhood dream. In later life he finds that real happiness is not to be found in just trying to be a number one man, or even a first-rater in the heartbreaking struggle for money, romance, or self-importance. He learns that he can be content as long as he plays well whatever cards life deals him. He's still ambitious, but not absurdly so, because he can now see and accept actual reality. He's willing to stay right size.

But not so with alcoholics. When A.A. was quite young, a number of eminent psychologists and doctors made an exhaustive study of a good-sized group of so-called problem drinkers. The doctors weren't trying to find how different we were from one another; they sought to find whatever personality traits, if any, this group of alcoholics had in common. They finally came up with a conclusion that shocked the A.A. members of that time. These distinguished men had the nerve to say that most of the alcoholics under investigation were still childish, emotionally sensitive, and grandiose.

How we alcoholics did resent that verdict! We would not believe that our adult dreams were often truly childish. And considering the rough deal life had given us, we felt it perfectly natural that we were sensitive. As to our grandiose behavior, we insisted that we had been possessed of nothing but a high and legitimate ambition to win the battle of life.

In the years since, however, most of us have come to agree with those doctors. We have had a much keener look at ourselves and those about us. We have seen that we were prodded by unreasonable fears or anxieties into making a life business of winning fame, money, and what we thought was leadership. So false pride became the reverse side of that ruinous coin marked "Fear." We simply had to be number one people to cover up our deep-lying inferiorities. In fitful successes we boasted of greater feats to be done; in defeat we were bitter. If we didn't have much of any worldly success we became depressed and cowed. Then people said we were of the "inferior" type. But now we see ourselves as chips off the same old block. At heart we had all been abnormally fearful. It mattered little whether we had sat on the shore of life drinking ourselves into forgetfulness or had plunged in recklessly and willfully beyond our depth and ability. The result was the same—all of us had nearly perished in a sea of alcohol.

But today, in well-matured A.A.'s, these distorted drives have been restored to something like their true purpose and direction. We no longer strive to dominate or rule those about us in order to gain self-importance. We no longer seek fame and honor in order to be praised. When by devoted service to family, friends, business, or community we attract widespread affection and are sometimes singled out for posts of greater responsibility and trust, we try to be humbly grateful and exert ourselves the more in a spirit of love and service. True leadership, we find, depends upon able example and not upon vain displays of power or glory.

Still more wonderful is the feeling that we do not have to be specially distinguished among our fellows in order to be useful and profoundly happy. Not many of us can be leaders of prominence, nor do we wish to be. Service, gladly rendered, obligations squarely met, troubles well accepted or solved with God's help, the knowledge that at home or in the world outside we are partners in a common effort, the well-understood fact that in God's sight all human beings are important, the proof that love freely given surely brings a full return, the certainty that we are no longer isolated and alone in self-constructed prisons, the surety that we need no longer be square pegs in round holes but can fit and belong in God's scheme of things—these are the permanent and legitimate satisfactions of right living for which no amount of pomp and circumstance, no heap of material possessions, could possibly be substitutes. True ambition is not what we thought it was. True ambition is the deep desire to live usefully and walk humbly under the grace of God.

These little studies of A.A.'s Twelve Steps now come to a close. We have been considering so many problems that it may appear that A.A. consists mainly of racking dilemmas and troubleshooting. To a certain extent, that is true. We have been talking about problems because we are problem people who have found a way up and out, and who wish to share our knowledge of that way with all who can use it. For it is only by accepting and solving our problems that we can begin to get right with ourselves and with the world about us, and with Him who presides over us all. Understanding is the key to right principles and attitudes, and right action is the key to good living; therefore the joy of good living is the theme of A.A.'s Twelfth Step.

With each passing day of our lives, may every one of us sense more deeply the inner meaning of A.A.'s simple prayer:

God grant us the serenity to accept the things we cannot change,
Courage to change the things we can,
And wisdom to know the difference.

THE TWELVE TRADITIONS

Tradition One

"Our common welfare should come first; personal recovery depends upon A.A. unity."

THE unity of Alcoholics Anonymous is the most cherished quality our Society has. Our lives, the lives of all to come, depend squarely upon it. We stay whole, or A.A. dies. Without unity, the heart of A.A. would cease to beat; our world arteries would no longer carry the life-giving grace of God; His gift to us would be spent aimlessly. Back again in their caves, alcoholics would reproach us and say, "What a great thing A.A. might have been!"

"Does this mean," some will anxiously ask, "that in A.A. the individual doesn't count for much? Is he to be dominated by his group and swallowed up in it?"

We may certainly answer this question with a loud "No!" We believe there isn't a fellowship on earth which lavishes more devoted care upon its individual members; surely there is none which more jealously guards the individual's right to think, talk, and act as he wishes. No A.A. can compel another to do anything; nobody can be punished or expelled. Our Twelve Steps to recovery are suggestions; the Twelve Traditions which guarantee A.A.'s unity contain not a single "Don't." They repeatedly say "We ought..." but never "You must!"

To many minds all this liberty for the individual spells sheer anarchy. Every newcomer, every friend who looks at

A.A. for the first time is greatly puzzled. They see liberty verging on license, yet they recognize at once that A.A. has an irresistible strength of purpose and action. "How," they ask, "can such a crowd of anarchists function at all? How can they possibly place their common welfare first? What in Heaven's name holds them together?"

Those who look closely soon have the key to this strange paradox. The A.A. member has to conform to the principles of recovery. His life actually depends upon obedience to spiritual principles. If he deviates too far, the penalty is sure and swift; he sickens and dies. At first he goes along because he must, but later he discovers a way of life he really wants to live. Moreover, he finds he cannot keep this priceless gift unless he gives it away. Neither he nor anybody else can survive unless he carries the A.A. message. The moment this Twelfth Step work forms a group, another discovery is made—that most individuals cannot recover unless there *is* a group. Realization dawns that he is but a small part of a great whole; that no personal sacrifice is too great for preservation of the Fellowship. He learns that the clamor of desires and ambitions within him must be silenced whenever these could damage the group. It becomes plain that the group must survive or the individual will not.

So at the outset, how best to live and work together as groups became the prime question. In the world about us we saw personalities destroying whole peoples. The struggle for wealth, power, and prestige was tearing humanity apart as never before. If strong people were stalemated in the search for peace and harmony, what was to become of our erratic band of alcoholics? As we had once struggled and prayed for individual recovery, just so earnestly did we commence to quest for the principles through which A.A. itself might survive. On anvils of experience, the structure of our Society was hammered out.

Countless times, in as many cities and hamlets, we reenacted the story of Eddie Rickenbacker and his courageous company when their plane crashed in the Pacific. Like us, they had suddenly found themselves saved from death, but still floating upon a perilous sea. How well *they* saw that their common welfare came first. None might become selfish of water or bread. Each needed to consider the others, and in abiding faith they knew they must find their real strength. And this they did find, in measure to transcend all the defects of their frail craft, every test of uncertainty, pain, fear, and despair, and even the death of one.

Thus has it been with A.A. By faith and by works we have been able to build upon the lessons of an incredible experience. They live today in the Twelve Traditions of Alcoholics Anonymous, which—God willing—shall sustain us in unity for so long as He may need us.

Tradition Two

"For our group purpose there is but one ultimate authority—a loving God as He may express Himself in our group conscience. Our leaders are but trusted servants; they do not govern."

WHERE does A.A. get its direction? Who runs it? This, too, is a puzzler for every friend and newcomer. When told that our Society has no president having authority to govern it, no treasurer who can compel the payment of any dues, no board of directors who can cast an erring member into outer darkness, when indeed no A.A. can give another a directive and enforce obedience, our friends gasp and exclaim, "This simply can't be. There must be an angle somewhere." These practical folk then read Tradition Two, and learn that the sole authority in A.A. is a loving God as He may express Himself in the group conscience. They dubiously ask an experienced A.A. member if this really works. The member, sane to all appearances, immediately answers, "Yes! It definitely does." The friends mutter that this looks vague, nebulous, pretty naive to them. Then they commence to watch us with speculative eyes, pick up a fragment of A.A. history, and soon have the solid facts.

What are these facts of A.A. life which brought us to this apparently impractical principle?

John Doe, a good A.A., moves—let us say—to Middletown, U.S.A. Alone now, he reflects that he may not be able to stay sober, or even alive, unless he passes on to other alcoholics what was so freely given him. He feels a spiritual and ethical compulsion, because hundreds may be suffering within reach of his help. Then, too, he misses his home group. He needs other alcoholics as much as they need him. He visits preachers, doctors, editors, policemen, and bartenders …with the result that Middletown now has a group, and he is the founder.

Being the founder, he is at first the boss. Who else could be? Very soon, though, his assumed authority to run everything begins to be shared with the first alcoholics he has helped. At this moment, the benign dictator becomes the chairman of a committee composed of his friends. These are the growing group's hierarchy of service—self-appointed, of course, because there is no other way. In a matter of months, A.A. booms in Middletown.

The founder and his friends channel spirituality to newcomers, hire halls, make hospital arrangements, and entreat their wives to brew gallons of coffee. Being on the human side, the founder and his friends may bask a little in glory. They say to one another, "Perhaps it would be a good idea if we continue to keep a firm hand on A.A. in this town. After all, we are experienced. Besides, look at all the good we've done these drunks. They should be grateful!" True, founders and their friends are sometimes wiser and more humble than this. But more often at this stage they are not.

Growing pains now beset the group. Panhandlers panhandle. Lonely hearts pine. Problems descend like an avalanche. Still more important, murmurs are heard in the body politic, which swell into a loud cry: "Do these oldtimers think they can run this group forever? Let's have an election!" The founder and his friends are hurt and depressed. They rush from crisis to crisis and from member to member, pleading; but it's no use, the revolution is on. The group conscience is about to take over.

Now comes the election. If the founder and his friends have served well, they may—to their surprise—be reinstated for a time. If, however, they have heavily resisted the rising tide of democracy, they may be summarily beached. In either case, the group now has a so-called rotating committee, very sharply limited in its authority. In no sense whatever can its members govern or direct the group. They are servants. Theirs is the sometimes thankless privilege of doing the group's chores. Headed by the chairman, they look after public relations and arrange meetings. Their treasurer, strictly accountable, takes money from the hat that is passed, banks it, pays the rent and other bills, and makes a regular report at business meetings. The secretary sees that literature is on the table, looks after the phone-answering service, answers the mail, and sends out notices of meetings. Such are the simple services that enable the group to function. The committee gives no spiritual advice, judges no one's conduct, issues no orders. Every one of them may be promptly eliminated at the next election if they try this. And so they make the belated discovery that they are really servants, not senators. These are universal experiences. Thus throughout A.A. does the group conscience decree the terms upon which its leaders shall serve.

This brings us straight to the question "Does A.A. have a real leadership?" Most emphatically the answer is "Yes,

notwithstanding the apparent lack of it." Let's turn again
to the deposed founder and his friends. What becomes of
them? As their grief and anxiety wear away, a subtle change
begins. Ultimately, they divide into two classes known in
A.A. slang as "elder statesmen" and "bleeding deacons."
The elder statesman is the one who sees the wisdom of the
group's decision, who holds no resentment over his reduced
status, whose judgment, fortified by considerable experience, is sound, and who is willing to sit quietly on the side-
lines patiently awaiting developments. The bleeding deacon
is one who is just as surely convinced that the group cannot
get along without him, who constantly connives for reelec-
tion to office, and who continues to be consumed with self-
pity. A few hemorrhage so badly that—drained of all A.A.
spirit and principle—they get drunk. At times the A.A.
landscape seems to be littered with bleeding forms. Nearly
every oldtimer in our Society has gone through this process
in some degree. Happily, most of them survive and live to
become elder statesmen. They become the real and permanent leadership of A.A. Theirs is the quiet opinion, the
sure knowledge and humble example that resolve a crisis.
When sorely perplexed, the group inevitably turns to them
for advice. They become the voice of the group conscience;
in fact, these are the true voice of Alcoholics Anonymous.
They do not drive by mandate; they lead by example. This
is the experience which has led us to the conclusion that
our group conscience, well-advised by its elders, will be in
the long run wiser than any single leader.

When A.A. was only three years old, an event occurred
demonstrating this principle. One of the first members of

A.A., entirely contrary to his own desires, was obliged to conform to group opinion. Here is the story in his words.

"One day I was doing a Twelfth Step job at a hospital in New York. The proprietor, Charlie, summoned me to his office. 'Bill,' he said, 'I think it's a shame that you are financially so hard up. All around you these drunks are getting well and making money. But you're giving this work full time, and you're broke. It isn't fair.' Charlie fished in his desk and came up with an old financial statement. Handing it to me, he continued, 'This shows the kind of money the hospital used to make back in the 1920's. Thousands of dollars a month. It should be doing just as well now, and it would—if only you'd help me. So why don't you move your work in here? I'll give you an office, a decent drawing account, and a very healthy slice of the profits. Three years ago, when my head doctor, Silkworth, began to tell me of the idea of helping drunks by spirituality, I thought it was crackpot stuff, but I've changed my mind. Some day this bunch of ex-drunks of yours will fill Madison Square Garden, and I don't see why you should starve meanwhile. What I propose is perfectly ethical. You can become a lay therapist, and more successful than anybody in the business.'

"I was bowled over. There were a few twinges of conscience until I saw how really ethical Charlie's proposal was. There was nothing wrong whatever with becoming a lay therapist. I thought of Lois coming home exhausted from the department store each day, only to cook supper for a houseful of drunks who weren't paying board. I thought of the large sum of money still owing my Wall Street creditors. I thought of a few of my alcoholic friends, who were making as much money as ever. Why shouldn't I do as well as they?

"Although I asked Charlie for a little time to consider it, my own mind was about made up. Racing back to Brooklyn on the subway, I had a seeming flash of divine guidance. It was only a single sentence, but most convincing. In fact, it came right out of the Bible—a voice kept saying to me, 'The laborer is worthy of his hire.' Arriving home, I found Lois cooking as usual, while three drunks looked hungrily on from the kitchen door. I drew her aside and told the glorious news. She looked interested, but not as excited as I thought she should be.

"It was meeting night. Although none of the alcoholics we boarded seemed to get sober, some others had. With their wives they crowded into our downstairs parlor. At once I burst into the story of my opportunity. Never shall I forget their impassive faces, and the steady gaze they focused upon me. With waning enthusiasm, my tale trailed off to the end. There was a long silence.

"Almost timidly, one of my friends began to speak. 'We know how hard up you are, Bill. It bothers us a lot. We've often wondered what we might do about it. But I think I speak for everyone here when I say that what you now propose bothers us an awful lot more.' The speaker's voice grew more confident. 'Don't you realize,' he went on, 'that you can never become a professional? As generous as Charlie has been to us, don't you see that we can't tie this thing up with his hospital or any other? You tell us that Charlie's proposal is ethical. Sure, it's ethical, but what we've got won't run on ethics only; it has to be better.

Sure, Charlie's idea is good, but it isn't good enough. This is a matter of life and death, Bill, and nothing but the very best will do!' Challengingly, my friends looked at me as their spokesman continued. 'Bill, haven't you often said right here in this meeting that sometimes the good is the enemy of the best? Well, this is a plain case of it. You can't do this thing to us!'

"So spoke the group conscience. The group was right and I was wrong; the voice on the subway was not the voice of God. Here was the true voice, welling up out of my friends. I listened, and—thank God—I obeyed."

Tradition Three

"The only requirement for A.A. membership is a desire to stop drinking."

THIS Tradition is packed with meaning. For A.A. is really saying to every serious drinker, "You are an A.A. member if *you* say so. You can declare yourself in; nobody can keep you out. No matter who you are, no matter how low you've gone, no matter how grave your emotional complications—even your crimes—we still can't deny you A.A. We don't *want* to keep you out. We aren't a bit afraid you'll harm us, never mind how twisted or violent you may be. We just want to be sure that you get the same great chance for sobriety that we've had. So you're an A.A. member the minute you declare yourself."

To establish this principle of membership took years of harrowing experience. In our early time, nothing seemed so fragile, so easily breakable as an A.A. group. Hardly an alcoholic we approached paid any attention; most of those who did join us were like flickering candles in a windstorm. Time after time, their uncertain flames blew out and couldn't be relighted. Our unspoken, constant thought was "Which of us may be the next?"

A member gives us a vivid glimpse of those days. "At one time," he says, "every A.A. group had many membership rules. Everybody was scared witless that something or somebody would capsize the boat and dump us all back

into the drink. Our Foundation office* asked each group to
send in its list of 'protective' regulations. The total list was
a mile long. If all those rules had been in effect everywhere,
nobody could have possibly joined A.A. at all, so great was
the sum of our anxiety and fear.

"We were resolved to admit nobody to A.A. but that
hypothetical class of people we termed 'pure alcoholics.'
Except for their guzzling, and the unfortunate results there-
of, they could have no other complications. So beggars,
tramps, asylum inmates, prisoners, queers, plain crackpots,
and fallen women were definitely out. Yes sir, we'd cater
only to pure and respectable alcoholics! Any others would
surely destroy us. Besides, if we took in those odd ones,
what would decent people say about us? We built a fine-
mesh fence right around A.A.

"Maybe this sounds comical now. Maybe you think we
oldtimers were pretty intolerant. But I can tell you there
was nothing funny about the situation then. We were grim
because we felt our lives and homes were threatened, and
that was no laughing matter. Intolerant, you say? Well, we
were frightened. Naturally, we began to act like most everybody does when afraid. After all, isn't fear the true basis
of intolerance? Yes, we were intolerant."

How could we then guess that all those fears were to
prove groundless? How could we know that thousands of
these sometimes frightening people were to make aston-
ishing recoveries and become our greatest workers and

---

* In 1954, the name of the Alcoholic Foundation, Inc., was changed to the General
Service Board of Alcoholics Anonymous, Inc., and the Foundation office is now
the General Service Office.

intimate friends? Was it credible that A.A. was to have a divorce rate far lower than average? Could we then foresee that troublesome people were to become our principal teachers of patience and tolerance? Could any then imagine a society which would include every conceivable kind of character, and cut across every barrier of race, creed, politics, and language with ease?

Why did A.A. finally drop all its membership regulations? Why did we leave it to each newcomer to decide himself whether he was an alcoholic and whether he should join us? Why did we dare to say, contrary to the experience of society and government everywhere, that we would neither punish nor deprive any A.A. of membership, that we must never compel anyone to pay anything, believe anything, or conform to anything?

The answer, now seen in Tradition Three, was simplicity itself. At last experience taught us that to take away any alcoholic's full chance was sometimes to pronounce his death sentence, and often to condemn him to endless misery. Who dared to be judge, jury, and executioner of his own sick brother?

As group after group saw these possibilities, they finally abandoned all membership regulations. One dramatic experience after another clinched this determination until it became our universal tradition. Here are two examples:

On the A.A. calendar it was Year Two. In that time nothing could be seen but two struggling, nameless groups of alcoholics trying to hold their faces up to the light.

A newcomer appeared at one of these groups, knocked on the door and asked to be let in. He talked frankly with that group's oldest member. He soon proved that his was a desperate case, and that above all he wanted to get well. "But," he asked, "will you let me join your group? Since I am the victim of another addiction even worse stigmatized than alcoholism, you may not want me among you. Or will you?"

There was the dilemma. What should the group do? The oldest member summoned two others, and in confidence laid the explosive facts in their laps. Said he, "Well, what about it? If we turn this man away, he'll soon die. If we allow him in, only God knows what trouble he'll brew. What shall the answer be—yes or no?"

At first the elders could look only at the objections. "We deal," they said, "with alcoholics only. Shouldn't we sacrifice this one for the sake of the many?" So went the discussion while the newcomer's fate hung in the balance. Then one of the three spoke in a very different voice. "What we are really afraid of," he said, "is our reputation. We are much more afraid of what people might say than the trouble this strange alcoholic might bring. As we've been talking, five short words have been running through my mind. Something keeps repeating to me, 'What would the Master do?'" Not another word was said. What more indeed *could* be said?

Overjoyed, the newcomer plunged into Twelfth Step work. Tirelessly he laid A.A.'s message before scores of people. Since this was a very early group, those scores have since multiplied themselves into thousands. Never did he trouble anyone with his other difficulty. A.A. had taken its first step in the formation of Tradition Three.

Not long after the man with the double stigma knocked for admission, A.A.'s other group received into its membership a salesman we shall call Ed. A power driver, this one, and brash as any salesman could possibly be. He had at least an idea a minute on how to improve A.A. These ideas he sold to fellow members with the same burning enthusiasm with which he distributed automobile polish. But he had one idea that wasn't so salable. Ed was an atheist. His pet obsession was that A.A. could get along better without its "God nonsense." He browbeat everybody, and everybody expected that he'd soon get drunk—for at the time, you see, A.A. was on the pious side. There must be a heavy penalty, it was thought, for blasphemy. Distressingly enough, Ed proceeded to stay sober.

At length the time came for him to speak in a meeting. We shivered, for we knew what was coming. He paid a fine tribute to the Fellowship; he told how his family had been reunited; he extolled the virtue of honesty; he recalled the joys of Twelfth Step work; and then he lowered the boom. Cried Ed, "I can't stand this God stuff! It's a lot of malarkey for weak folks. This group doesn't need it, and I won't have it! To hell with it!"

A great wave of outraged resentment engulfed the meeting, sweeping every member to a single resolve: "Out he goes!"

The elders led Ed aside. They said firmly, "You can't talk like this around here. You'll have to quit it or get out." With great sarcasm Ed came back at them. "Now do tell! Is that so?" He reached over to a bookshelf and took up a sheaf of papers. On top of them lay the foreword to the book "Alcoholics Anonymous," then under preparation. He read aloud, "The only requirement for A.A. membership is a desire to stop drinking." Relentlessly, Ed went on, "When you guys wrote that sentence, did you mean it, or didn't you?"

Dismayed, the elders looked at one another, for they knew he had them cold. So Ed stayed.

Ed not only stayed, he stayed sober—month after month. The longer he kept dry, the louder he talked—against God. The group was in anguish so deep that all fraternal charity had vanished. "When, oh when," groaned members to one another, "will that guy get drunk?"

Quite a while later, Ed got a sales job which took him out of town. At the end of a few days, the news came in. He'd sent a telegram for money, and everybody knew what *that* meant! Then he got on the phone. In those days, we'd go anywhere on a Twelfth Step job, no matter how unpromising. But this time nobody stirred. "Leave him alone! Let him try it by himself for once; maybe he'll learn a lesson!"

About two weeks later, Ed stole by night into an A.A. member's house and, unknown to the family, went to bed. Daylight found the master of the house and another friend drinking their morning coffee. A noise was heard on the stairs. To their consternation, Ed appeared. A quizzical smile on his lips, he said, "Have you fellows had your morning meditation?" They quickly sensed that he was quite in earnest. In fragments, his story came out.

In a neighboring state, Ed had holed up in a cheap hotel. After all his pleas for help had been rebuffed, these words rang in his fevered mind: "They have deserted me. I have been deserted by my own kind. This is the end …nothing is left." As he tossed on his bed, his hand brushed the bureau near by, touching a book. Opening the book, he read. It was a Gideon Bible. Ed never confided any more of what he saw and felt in that hotel room. It was the year 1938. He hasn't had a drink since.

Nowadays, when oldtimers who know Ed foregather, they exclaim, "What if we had actually succeeded in throwing Ed out for blasphemy? What would have happened to him and all the others he later helped?"

So the hand of Providence early gave us a sign that any alcoholic is a member of our Society when *he* says so.

Tradition Four

"Each group should be autonomous except in matters affecting other groups or A.A. as a whole."

AUTONOMY is a ten-dollar word. But in relation to us, it means very simply that every A.A. group can manage its affairs exactly as it pleases, except when A.A. as a whole is threatened. Comes now the same question raised in Tradition One. Isn't such liberty foolishly dangerous?

Over the years, every conceivable deviation from our Twelve Steps and Traditions has been tried. That was sure to be, since we are so largely a band of ego-driven individualists. Children of chaos, we have defiantly played with every brand of fire, only to emerge unharmed and, we think, wiser. These very deviations created a vast process of trial and error which, under the grace of God, has brought us to where we stand today.

When A.A.'s Traditions were first published, in 1946, we had become sure that an A.A. group could stand almost any amount of battering. We saw that the group, exactly like the individual, must eventually conform to whatever tested principles would guarantee survival. We had discovered that there was perfect safety in the process of trial and error. So confident of this had we become that the original statement of A.A. tradition carried this significant sentence: "Any two or three alcoholics gathered together for sobriety may call themselves an A.A. group provided that as a group they have no other affiliation."

This meant, of course, that we had been given the courage to declare each A.A. group an individual entity, strictly reliant on its own conscience as a guide to action. In charting this enormous expanse of freedom, we found it necessary to post only two storm signals: A group ought not do anything which would greatly injure A.A. as a whole, nor ought it affiliate itself with anything or anybody else. There would be real danger should we commence to call some groups "wet," others "dry," still others "Republican" or "Communist," and yet others "Catholic" or "Protestant." The A.A. group would have to stick to its course or be hopelessly lost. Sobriety had to be its sole objective. In all other respects there was perfect freedom of will and action. Every group had the right to be wrong.

When A.A. was still young, lots of eager groups were forming. In a town we'll call Middleton, a real crackerjack had started up. The townspeople were as hot as firecrackers about it. Stargazing, the elders dreamed of innovations. They figured the town needed a great big alcoholic center, a kind of pilot plant A.A. groups could duplicate everywhere. Beginning on the ground floor there would be a club; in the second story they would sober up drunks and hand them currency for their back debts; the third deck would house an educational project—quite noncontroversial, of course. In imagination the gleaming center was to go up several stories more, but three would do for a start. This would all take a lot of money—other people's money. Believe it or not, wealthy townsfolk bought the idea.

There were, though, a few conservative dissenters among the alcoholics. They wrote the Foundation*, A.A.'s headquarters in New York, wanting to know about this sort of streamlining. They understood that the elders, just to nail things down good, were about to apply to the Foundation for a charter. These few were disturbed and skeptical.

Of course, there was a promoter in the deal—a superpromoter. By his eloquence he allayed all fears, despite advice from the Foundation that it could issue no charter, and that ventures which mixed an A.A. group with medication and education had come to sticky ends elsewhere. To make things safer, the promoter organized three corporations and became president of them all. Freshly painted, the new center shone. The warmth of it all spread through the town. Soon things began to hum. To insure foolproof, continuous operation, sixty-one rules and regulations were adopted.

But alas, this bright scene was not long in darkening. Confusion replaced serenity. It was found that some drunks yearned for education, but doubted if they were alcoholics. The personality defects of others could be cured maybe with a loan. Some were club-minded, but it was just a question of taking care of the lonely heart. Sometimes the swarming applicants would go for all three floors. Some would start at the top and come through to the bottom, becoming club members; others started in the club, pitched a binge, were hospitalized, then graduated to education on the third floor. It was a beehive of activity, all right, but

---

* In 1954, the name of the Alcoholic Foundation, Inc., was changed to the General Service Board of Alcoholics Anonymous, Inc., and the Foundation office is now the General Service Office.

unlike a beehive, it was confusion compounded. An A.A. group, as such, simply couldn't handle this sort of project. All too late that was discovered. Then came the inevitable explosion—something like that day the boiler burst in Wombley's Clapboard Factory. A chill chokedamp of fear and frustration fell over the group.

When that lifted, a wonderful thing had happened. The head promoter wrote the Foundation office. He said he wished he'd paid some attention to A.A. experience. Then he did something else that was to become an A.A. classic. It all went on a little card about golf-score size. The cover read: "Middleton Group #1, Rule #62." Once the card was unfolded, a single pungent sentence leaped to the eye: "Don't take yourself too damn seriously."

Thus it was that under Tradition Four an A.A. group had exercised its right to be wrong. Moreover, it had performed a great service for Alcoholics Anonymous, because it had been humbly willing to apply the lessons it learned. It had picked itself up with a laugh and gone on to better things. Even the chief architect, standing in the ruins of his dream, could laugh at himself—and that is the very acme of humility.

Tradition Five

*"Each group has but one primary purpose—
to carry its message to the alcoholic who
still suffers."*

"SHOEMAKER, stick to thy last!" …better do one thing
supremely well than many badly. That is the central theme
of this Tradition. Around it our Society gathers in unity.
The very life of our Fellowship requires the preservation
of this principle.

Alcoholics Anonymous can be likened to a group of phy-
sicians who might find a cure for cancer, and upon whose
concerted work would depend the answer for sufferers of
this disease. True, each physician in such a group might
have his own specialty. Every doctor concerned would at
times wish he could devote himself to his chosen field rather than work only with the group. But once these men had
hit upon a cure, once it became apparent that only by their
united effort could this be accomplished, then all of them
would feel bound to devote themselves solely to the relief
of cancer. In the radiance of such a miraculous discovery,
any doctor would set his other ambitions aside, at whatever
personal cost.

Just as firmly bound by obligation are the members
of Alcoholics Anonymous, who have demonstrated that
they can help problem drinkers as others seldom can. The
unique ability of each A.A. to identify himself with, and

bring recovery to, the newcomer in no way depends upon his learning, eloquence, or on any special individual skills. The only thing that matters is that he is an alcoholic who has found a key to sobriety. These legacies of suffering and of recovery are easily passed among alcoholics, one to the other. This is our gift from God, and its bestowal upon others like us is the one aim that today animates A.A.'s all around the globe.

There is another reason for this singleness of purpose. It is the great paradox of A.A. that we know we can seldom keep the precious gift of sobriety unless we give it away. If a group of doctors possessed a cancer cure, they might be conscience-stricken if they failed their mission through self-seeking. Yet such a failure wouldn't jeopardize their personal survival. For us, if we neglect those who are still sick, there is unremitting danger to our own lives and sanity. Under these compulsions of self-preservation, duty, and love, it is not strange that our Society has concluded that it has but one high mission—to carry the A.A. message to those who don't know there's a way out.

Highlighting the wisdom of A.A.'s single purpose, a member tells this story:

"Restless one day, I felt I'd better do some Twelfth Step work. Maybe I should take out some insurance against a slip. But first I'd have to find a drunk to work on.

"So I hopped the subway to Towns Hospital, where I asked Dr. Silkworth if he had a prospect. 'Nothing too promising,' the little doc said. 'There's just one chap on the third floor who might be a possibility. But he's an awfully tough Irishman. I never saw a man so obstinate. He shouts that if his partner would treat him better, and his wife would leave him alone, he'd soon solve his alcohol problem. He's had a bad case of D.T.'s, he's pretty foggy, and he's very suspicious of everybody. Doesn't sound too good, does it? But working with him may do something for you, so why don't you have a go at it?'

"I was soon sitting beside a big hulk of a man. Decidedly unfriendly, he stared at me out of eyes which were slits in his red and swollen face. I had to agree with the doctor—he certainly didn't look good. But I told him my own story. I explained what a wonderful Fellowship we had, how well we understood each other. I bore down hard on the hopelessness of the drunk's dilemma. I insisted that few drunks could ever get well on their own steam, but that in our groups we could do together what we could not do separately. He interrupted to scoff at this and asserted he'd fix his wife, his partner, and his alcoholism by himself. Sarcastically he asked, 'How much does your scheme cost?'

"I was thankful I could tell him, 'Nothing at all.'

"His next question: 'What are *you* getting out of it?'

"Of course, my answer was 'My own sobriety and a mighty happy life.'

"Still dubious, he demanded, 'Do you really mean the only reason you are here is to try and help me and to help yourself?'

"'Yes,' I said. 'That's absolutely all there is to it. There's no angle.'

"Then, hesitantly, I ventured to talk about the spiritual side of our program. What a freeze that drunk gave me! I'd no sooner got the word 'spiritual' out of my mouth than he pounced. 'Oh!' he said. 'Now I get it! You're proselyting for some damn religious sect or other. Where do you get that "no angle" stuff? I belong to a great church that means everything to me. You've got a nerve to come in here talking religion!'

"Thank heaven I came up with the right answer for that one. It was based foursquare on the single purpose of A.A. 'You have faith,' I said. 'Perhaps far deeper faith than mine. No doubt you're better taught in religious matters than I. So I can't tell you anything about religion. I don't even want to try. I'll bet, too, that you could give me a letter-perfect definition of humility. But from what you've told me about yourself and your problems and how you propose to lick them, I think I know what's wrong.'

"'Okay,' he said. 'Give me the business.'

"'Well,' said I, 'I think you're just a conceited Irishman who thinks he can run the whole show.'

"This really rocked him. But as he calmed down, he began to listen while I tried to show him that humility was the main key to sobriety. Finally, he saw that I wasn't attempting to change his religious views, that I wanted him to find the grace in his own religion that would aid his recovery. From there on we got along fine.

"Now," concludes the oldtimer, "suppose I'd been obliged to talk to this man on religious grounds? Suppose my answer had to be that A.A. needed a lot of money; that A.A. went in for education, hospitals, and rehabilitation? Suppose I'd suggested that I'd take a hand in his domestic and business affairs? Where would we have wound up? No place, of course."

Years later, this tough Irish customer liked to say, "My sponsor sold me one idea, and that was sobriety. At the time, I couldn't have bought anything else."

Tradition Six

"An A.A. group ought never endorse, finance, or lend the A.A. name to any related facility or outside enterprise, lest problems of money, property, and prestige divert us from our primary purpose."

THE moment we saw that we had an answer for alcoholism, it was reasonable (or so it seemed at the time) for us to feel that we might have the answer to a lot of other things. The A.A. groups, many thought, could go into business, might finance any enterprise whatever in the total field of alcoholism. In fact, we felt duty-bound to throw the whole weight of the A.A. name behind any meritorious cause.

Here are some of the things we dreamed. Hospitals didn't like alcoholics, so we thought we'd build a hospital chain of our own. People needed to be told what alcoholism was, so we'd educate the public, even rewrite school and medical textbooks. We'd gather up derelicts from skid rows, sort out those who could get well, and make it possible for the rest to earn their livelihood in a kind of quarantined confinement. Maybe these places would make large sums of money to carry on our other good works. We seriously thought of rewriting the laws of the land, and having it declared that alcoholics are sick people. No more would they be jailed; judges would parole them in our custody. We'd spill A.A. into the dark regions of dope addiction

and criminality. We'd form groups of depressive and para-
noid folks; the deeper the neurosis, the better we'd like it. It
stood to reason that if alcoholism could be licked, so could
any problem.

It occurred to us that we could take what we had into
the factories and cause laborers and capitalists to love each
other. Our uncompromising honesty might soon clean up
politics. With one arm around the shoulder of religion and
the other around the shoulder of medicine, we'd resolve
their differences. Having learned to live so happily, we'd
show everybody else how. Why, we thought, our Society of
Alcoholics Anonymous might prove to be the spearhead
of a new spiritual advance! We might transform the world.

Yes, we of A.A. did dream those dreams. How natural that was, since most alcoholics are bankrupt idealists.
Nearly every one of us had wished to do great good, perform great deeds, and embody great ideals. We are all per-
fectionists who, failing perfection, have gone to the other
extreme and settled for the bottle and the blackout. Providence, through A.A., had brought us within reach of our
highest expectations. So why shouldn't we share our way of
life with everyone?

Whereupon we tried A.A. hospitals—they all bogged
down because you cannot put an A.A. group into business;
too many busybody cooks spoil the broth. A.A. groups
had their fling at education, and when they began to publicly whoop up the merits of this or that brand, people became confused. Did A.A. fix drunks or was it an educational project? Was A.A. spiritual or was it medical? Was
it a reform movement? In consternation, we saw ourselves

getting married to all kinds of enterprises, some good and some not so good. Watching alcoholics committed willy-nilly to prisons or asylums, we began to cry, "There oughtta be a law!" A.A.'s commenced to thump tables in legislative committee rooms and agitated for legal reform. That made good newspaper copy, but little else. We saw we'd soon be mired in politics. Even inside A.A. we found it imperative to remove the A.A. name from clubs and Twelfth Step houses.

These adventures implanted a deep-rooted conviction that in no circumstances could we endorse any related enterprise, no matter how good. We of Alcoholics Anonymous could not be all things to all men, nor should we try.

Years ago this principle of "no endorsement" was put to a vital test. Some of the great distilling companies proposed to go into the field of alcohol education. It would be a good thing, they believed, for the liquor trade to show a sense of public responsibility. They wanted to say that liquor should be enjoyed, not misused; hard drinkers ought to slow down, and problem drinkers—alcoholics—should not drink at all.

In one of their trade associations, the question arose of just how this campaign should be handled. Of course, they would use the resources of radio, press, and films to make their point. But what kind of person should head the job? They immediately thought of Alcoholics Anonymous. If they could find a good public relations man in our ranks, why wouldn't he be ideal? He'd certainly know the problem. His connection with A.A. would be valuable, because the Fellowship stood high in public favor and hadn't an enemy in the world.

Soon they'd spotted their man, an A.A. with the necessary

experience. Straightway he appeared at New York's A.A. headquarters, asking, "Is there anything in our tradition that suggests I shouldn't take a job like this one? The kind of education seems good to me, and is not too controversial. Do you headquarters folks see any bugs in it?"

At first glance, it did look like a good thing. Then doubt crept in. The association wanted to use our member's full name in all its advertising; he was to be described both as its director of publicity and as a member of Alcoholics Anonymous. Of course, there couldn't be the slightest objection if such an association hired an A.A. member solely because of his public relations ability and his knowledge of alcoholism. But that wasn't the whole story, for in this case not only was an A.A. member to break his anonymity at a public level, he was to link the name Alcoholics Anonymous to this particular educational project in the minds of millions. It would be bound to appear that A.A. was now backing education—liquor trade association style.

The minute we saw this compromising fact for what it was, we asked the prospective publicity director how he felt about it. "Great guns!" he said. "Of course I can't take the job. The ink wouldn't be dry on the first ad before an awful shriek would go up from the dry camp. They'd be out with lanterns looking for an honest A.A. to plump for *their* brand of education. A.A. would land exactly in the middle of the wet-dry controversy. Half the people in this country would think we'd signed up with the drys, the other half would think we'd joined the wets. What a mess!"

"Nevertheless," we pointed out, "you still have a legal right to take this job."

"I know that," he said. "But this is no time for legalities. Alcoholics Anonymous saved my life, and it comes first. I certainly won't be the guy to land A.A. in big-time trouble, and this would really do it!"

Concerning endorsements, our friend had said it all. We saw as never before that we could not lend the A.A. name to any cause other than our own.

Tradition Seven

"Every A.A. group ought to be fully self-supporting, declining outside contributions."

SELF-SUPPORTING alcoholics? Who ever heard of such a thing? Yet we find that's what we have to be. This principle is telling evidence of the profound change that A.A. has wrought in all of us. Everybody knows that active alcoholics scream that they have no troubles money can't cure. Always, we've had our hands out. Time out of mind we've been dependent upon somebody, usually money-wise. When a society composed entirely of alcoholics says it's going to pay its bills, that's really news.

Probably no A.A. Tradition had the labor pains this one did. In early times, we were all broke. When you add to this the habitual supposition that people ought to give money to alcoholics trying to stay sober, it can be understood why we thought we deserved a pile of folding money. What great things A.A. would be able to do with it! But oddly enough, people who had money thought otherwise. They figured that it was high time we now—sober—paid our own way. So our Fellowship stayed poor because it had to.

There was another reason for our collective poverty. It was soon apparent that while alcoholics would spend lavishly on Twelfth Step cases, they had a terrific aversion to dropping money into a meeting-place hat for group purposes. We were astounded to find that we were as tight as the bark on a tree. So A.A., the movement, started and stayed broke, while its individual members waxed prosperous.

Alcoholics are certainly all-or-nothing people. Our reactions to money prove this. As A.A. emerged from its infancy into adolescence, we swung from the idea that we needed vast sums of money to the notion that A.A. shouldn't have any. On every lip were the words "You can't mix A.A. and money. We shall have to separate the spiritual from the material." We took this violent new tack because here and there members had tried to make money out of their A.A. connections, and we feared we'd be exploited. Now and then, grateful benefactors had endowed clubhouses, and as a result there was sometimes outside interference in our affairs. We had been presented with a hospital, and almost immediately the donor's son became its principal patient and would-be manager. One A.A. group was given five thousand dollars to do with what it would. The hassle over that chunk of money played havoc for years. Frightened by these complications, some groups refused to have a cent in their treasuries.

Despite these misgivings, we had to recognize the fact that A.A. had to function. Meeting places cost something. To save whole areas from turmoil, small offices had to be set up, telephones installed, and a few full-time secretaries hired. Over many protests, these things were accomplished. We saw that if they weren't, the man coming in the door couldn't get a break. These simple services would require small sums of money which we could and would pay ourselves. At last the pendulum stopped swinging and pointed straight at Tradition Seven as it reads today.

In this connection, Bill likes to tell the following pointed story. He explains that when Jack Alexander's *Saturday Evening Post* piece broke in 1941, thousands of frantic letters from distraught alcoholics and their families hit the Foundation[*] letterbox in New York. "Our office staff," Bill says, "consisted of two people: one devoted secretary and myself. How could this landslide of appeals be met? We'd have to have some more full-time help, that was sure. So we asked the A.A. groups for voluntary contributions. Would they send us a dollar a member a year? Otherwise this heartbreaking mail would have to go unanswered.

"To my surprise, the response of the groups was slow. I got mighty sore about it. Looking at this avalanche of mail one morning at the office, I paced up and down ranting how irresponsible and tightwad my fellow members were. Just then an old acquaintance stuck a tousled and aching head in the door. He was our prize slippee. I could see he had an awful hangover. Remembering some of my own, my heart filled with pity. I motioned him to my inside cubicle and produced a five-dollar bill. As my total income was thirty dollars a week at the time, this was a fairly large donation. Lois really needed the money for groceries, but that didn't stop me. The intense relief on my friend's face warmed my heart. I felt especially virtuous as I thought of all the ex-drunks who wouldn't even send the Foundation

---

[*] In 1954, the name of the Alcoholic Foundation, Inc., was changed to the General Service Board of Alcoholics Anonymous, Inc., and the Foundation office is now the General Service Office.

a dollar apiece, and here I was gladly making a five-dollar investment to fix a hangover.

"The meeting that night was at New York's old 24th Street Clubhouse. During the intermission, the treasurer gave a timid talk on how broke the club was. (That was in the period when you couldn't mix money and A.A.) But finally he said it—the landlord would put us out if we didn't pay up. He concluded his remarks by saying, 'Now boys, please go heavier on the hat tonight, will you?'

"I heard all this quite plainly, as I was piously trying to convert a newcomer who sat next to me. The hat came in my direction, and I reached into my pocket. Still working on my prospect, I fumbled and came up with a fifty-cent piece. Somehow it looked like a very big coin. Hastily, I dropped it back and fished out a dime, which clinked thinly as I dropped it in the hat. Hats never got folding money in those days.

"Then I woke up. I who had boasted my generosity that morning was treating my own club worse than the distant alcoholics who had forgotten to send the Foundation their dollars. I realized that my five-dollar gift to the slippee was an ego-feeding proposition, bad for him and bad for me. There *was* a place in A.A. where spirituality and money would mix, and that was in the hat!"

There is another story about money. One night in 1948, the trustees of the Foundation were having their quarterly meeting. The agenda discussion included a very important question. A certain lady had died. When her will was read, it was discovered she had left Alcoholics Anonymous in trust with the Alcoholic Foundation a sum of ten thousand dollars. The question was: Should A.A. take the gift?

What a debate we had on that one! The Foundation was really hard up just then; the groups weren't sending in enough for the support of the office; we had been tossing in all the book income and even that hadn't been enough. The reserve was melting like snow in springtime. We needed that ten thousand dollars. "Maybe," some said, "the groups will never fully support the office. We can't let it shut down; it's far too vital. Yes, let's take the money. Let's take all such donations in the future. We're going to need them."

Then came the opposition. They pointed out that the Foundation board already knew of a total of half a million dollars set aside for A.A. in the wills of people still alive. Heaven only knew how much there was we hadn't heard about. If outside donations weren't declined, absolutely cut off, then the Foundation would one day become rich. Moreover, at the slightest intimation to the general public from our trustees that we needed money, we could become immensely rich. Compared to this prospect, the ten thousand dollars under consideration wasn't much, but like the alcoholic's first drink it would, if taken, inevitably set up a disastrous chain reaction. Where would that land us? Whoever pays the piper is apt to call the tune, and if the A.A. Foundation obtained money from outside sources, its trustees might be tempted to run things without reference to the wishes of A.A. as a whole. Relieved of responsibility, every alcoholic would shrug and say, "Oh, the Foundation is wealthy—why should I bother?" The pressure of that fat treasury would surely tempt the board to invent all kinds of schemes to do good with such funds, and so divert A.A. from its primary purpose. The moment that happened, our Fellowship's confidence would be shaken. The board would be isolated, and would fall under heavy attack of criticism from both A.A. and the public. These were the possibilities, pro and con.

Then our trustees wrote a bright page of A.A. history. They declared for the principle that A.A. must always stay poor. Bare running expenses plus a prudent reserve would henceforth be the Foundation's financial policy. Difficult as it was, they officially declined that ten thousand dollars, and adopted a formal, airtight resolution that all such future gifts would be similarly declined. At that moment, we believe, the principle of corporate poverty was firmly and finally embedded in A.A. tradition.

When these facts were printed, there was a profound reaction. To people familiar with endless drives for charitable funds, A.A. presented a strange and refreshing spectacle. Approving editorials here and abroad generated a wave of confidence in the integrity of Alcoholics Anonymous. They pointed out that the irresponsible had become responsible, and that by making financial independence part of its tradition, Alcoholics Anonymous had revived an ideal that its era had almost forgotten.

Tradition Eight

"Alcoholics Anonymous should remain forever nonprofessional, but our service centers may employ special workers."

ALCOHOLICS ANONYMOUS will never have a professional class. We have gained some understanding of the ancient words "Freely ye have received, freely give." We have discovered that at the point of professionalism, money and spirituality do not mix. Almost no recovery from alcoholism has ever been brought about by the world's best professionals, whether medical or religious. We do not decry professionalism in other fields, but we accept the sober fact that it does not work for us. Every time we have tried to professionalize our Twelfth Step, the result has been exactly the same: Our single purpose has been defeated.

Alcoholics simply will not listen to a paid twelfth-stepper. Almost from the beginning, we have been positive that face-to-face work with the alcoholic who suffers could be based only on the desire to help and be helped. When an A.A. talks for money, whether at a meeting or to a single newcomer, it can have a very bad effect on him, too. The money motive compromises him and everything he says and does for his prospect. This has always been so obvious that only a very few A.A.'s have ever worked the Twelfth Step for a fee.

Despite this certainty, it is nevertheless true that few subjects have been the cause of more contention within our

Fellowship than professionalism. Caretakers who swept floors, cooks who fried hamburgers, secretaries in offices, authors writing books—all these we have seen hotly assailed because they were, as their critics angrily remarked, "making money out of A.A." Ignoring the fact that these labors were not Twelfth Step jobs at all, the critics attacked as A.A. professionals these workers of ours who were often doing thankless tasks that no one else could or would do. Even greater furors were provoked when A.A. members began to run rest homes and farms for alcoholics, when some hired out to corporations as personnel men in charge of the alcoholic problem in industry, when some became nurses on alcoholic wards, when others entered the field of alcohol education. In all these instances, and more, it was claimed that A.A. knowledge and experience were being sold for money, hence these people, too, were professionals.

At last, however, a plain line of cleavage could be seen between professionalism and nonprofessionalism. When we had agreed that the Twelfth Step couldn't be sold for money, we had been wise. But when we had declared that our Fellowship couldn't hire service workers nor could any A.A. member carry our knowledge into other fields, we were taking the counsel of fear, fear which today has been largely dispelled in the light of experience.

Take the case of the club janitor and cook. If a club is going to function, it has to be habitable and hospitable. We tried volunteers, who were quickly disenchanted with sweeping floors and brewing coffee seven days a week. They just didn't show up. Even more important, an empty club couldn't answer its telephone, but it was an open invitation to a drunk on a binge who possessed a spare key. So somebody had to look after the place full time. If we hired an alcoholic, he'd receive only what we'd have to pay a nonalcoholic for the same job. The job was not to *do* Twelfth Step work; it was to make Twelfth Step work possible. It was a service proposition, pure and simple.

Neither could A.A. itself function without full-time workers. At the Foundation* and intergroup offices, we couldn't employ nonalcoholics as secretaries; we had to have people who knew the A.A. pitch. But the minute we hired them, the ultraconservative and fearful ones shrilled, "Professionalism!" At one period, the status of these faithful servants was almost unbearable. They weren't asked to speak at A.A. meetings because they were "making money out of A.A." At times, they were actually shunned by fellow members. Even the charitably disposed described them as "a necessary evil." Committees took full advantage of this attitude to depress their salaries. They could regain some measure of virtue, it was thought, if they worked for A.A. real cheap. These notions persisted for years. Then we saw that if a hardworking secretary answered the phone dozens of times a day, listened to twenty wailing wives, arranged hospitalization and got sponsorship for ten newcomers, and was gently diplomatic with the irate drunk who complained about the job she was doing and how she was overpaid, then such a person could surely not be called a professional A.A. She was not professionaliz-

---

* In 1954, the name of the Alcoholic Foundation, Inc., was changed to the General Service Board of Alcoholics Anonymous, Inc., and the Foundation office is now the General Service Office.

ing the Twelfth Step; she was just making it possible. She was helping to give the man coming in the door the break he ought to have. Volunteer committeemen and assistants could be of great help, but they could not be expected to carry this load day in and day out.

At the Foundation, the same story repeats itself. Eight tons of books and literature per month do not package and channel themselves all over the world. Sacks of letters on every conceivable A.A. problem ranging from a lonely-heart Eskimo to the growing pains of thousands of groups must be answered by people who *know*. Right contacts with the world outside have to be maintained. A.A.'s lifelines have to be tended. So we hire A.A. staff members. We pay them well, and they earn what they get. They are professional secretaries,* but they certainly are not professional A.A.'s.

Perhaps the fear will always lurk in every A.A. heart that one day our name will be exploited by somebody for real cash. Even the suggestion of such a thing never fails to whip up a hurricane, and we have discovered that hurricanes have a way of mauling with equal severity both the just and the unjust. They are always unreasonable.

No individuals have been more buffeted by such emotional gusts than those A.A.'s bold enough to accept employment with outside agencies dealing with the alcohol problem. A university wanted an A.A. member to educate the public on alcoholism. A corporation wanted a person-

---

* The work of present-day staff members has no counterpart among the job categories of commercial organizations. These A.A.'s bring a wide range of business and professional experience to their service at the General Service Office.

nel man familiar with the subject. A state drunk farm wanted a manager who could really handle inebriates. A city
wanted an experienced social worker who understood what
alcohol could do to a family. A state alcohol commission
wanted a paid researcher. These are only a few of the jobs
which A.A. members as individuals have been asked to fill.
Now and then, A.A. members have bought farms or rest
homes where badly beat-up topers could find needed care.
The question was—and sometimes still is—are such activi-
ties to be branded as professionalism under A.A. tradition?

We think the answer is "No. Members who select such
full-time careers do not professionalize A.A.'s Twelfth
Step." The road to this conclusion was long and rocky.
At first, we couldn't see the real issue involved. In former
days, the moment an A.A. hired out to such enterprises,
he was immediately tempted to use the name Alcoholics Anonymous for publicity or money-raising purposes.
Drunk farms, educational ventures, state legislatures, and
commissions advertised the fact that A.A. members served
them. Unthinkingly, A.A.'s so employed recklessly broke
anonymity to thump the tub for their pet enterprise. For
this reason, some very good causes and all connected with
them suffered unjust criticism from A.A. groups. More
often than not, these onslaughts were spearheaded by the
cry "Professionalism! That guy is making money out of
A.A.!" Yet not a single one of them had been hired to do
A.A.'s Twelfth Step work. The violation in these instances
was not professionalism at all; it was breaking anonymity.
A.A.'s sole purpose was being compromised, and the name
of Alcoholics Anonymous was being misused.

It is significant, now that almost no A.A. in our Fellowship breaks anonymity at the public level, that nearly all these fears have subsided. We see that we have no right or need to discourage A.A.'s who wish to work as individuals in these wider fields. It would be actually antisocial were we to forbid them. We cannot declare A.A. such a closed corporation that we keep our knowledge and experience top secret. If an A.A. member acting as a citizen can become a better researcher, educator, personnel officer, then why not? Everybody gains, and we have lost nothing. True, some of the projects to which A.A.'s have attached themselves have been ill-conceived, but that makes not the slightest difference with the principle involved.

This is the exciting welter of events which has finally cast up A.A.'s Tradition of nonprofessionalism. Our Twelfth Step is never to be paid for, but those who labor in service for us are worthy of their hire.

Tradition Nine

"A.A., as such, ought never be organized; but we may create service boards or committees directly responsible to those they serve."

WHEN Tradition Nine was first written, it said that "Alcoholics Anonymous needs the least possible organization." In years since then, we have changed our minds about that. Today, we are able to say with assurance that Alcoholics Anonymous—A.A. as a whole—should never be organized at all. Then, in seeming contradiction, we proceed to create special service boards and committees which in themselves are organized. How, then, can we have an unorganized movement which can and does create a service organization for itself? Scanning this puzzler, people say, "What do they mean, no organization?"

Well, let's see. Did anyone ever hear of a nation, a church, a political party, even a benevolent association that had no membership rules? Did anyone ever hear of a society which couldn't somehow discipline its members and enforce obedience to necessary rules and regulations? Doesn't nearly every society on earth give authority to some of its members to impose obedience upon the rest and to punish or expel offenders? Therefore, every nation, in fact every form of society, has to be a government administered by human beings. Power to direct or govern is the essence of organization everywhere.

Yet Alcoholics Anonymous is an exception. It does not conform to this pattern. Neither its General Service Conference, its Foundation Board,* nor the humblest group committee can issue a single directive to an A.A. member and make it stick, let alone mete out any punishment. We've tried it lots of times, but utter failure is always the result. Groups have tried to expel members, but the banished have come back to sit in the meeting place, saying, "This is life for us; you can't keep us out." Committees have instructed many an A.A. to stop working on a chronic backslider, only to be told: "How I do my Twelfth Step work is my business. Who are you to judge?" This doesn't mean an A.A. won't take advice or suggestions from more experienced members, but he surely won't take orders. Who is more unpopular than the oldtime A.A., full of wisdom, who moves to another area and tries to tell the group there how to run its business? He and all like him who "view with alarm for the good of A.A." meet the most stubborn resistance or, worse still, laughter.

You might think A.A.'s headquarters in New York would be an exception. Surely, the people there would have to have some authority. But long ago, trustees and staff members alike found they could do no more than make suggestions, and very mild ones at that. They even had to coin a couple of sentences which still go into half the letters they write: "Of course, you are at perfect liberty to handle this matter any way you please. But the majority

---

* In 1954, the name of the Alcoholic Foundation, Inc., was changed to the General Service Board of Alcoholics Anonymous, Inc., and the Foundation office is now the General Service Office.

experience in A.A. does seem to suggest…" Now, that attitude is far removed from central government, isn't it? We recognize that alcoholics can't be dictated to—individually or collectively.

At this juncture, we can hear a churchman exclaim, "They are making disobedience a virtue!" He is joined by a psychiatrist who says, "Defiant brats! They won't grow up and conform to social usage!" The man in the street says, "I don't understand it. They must be nuts!" But all these observers have overlooked something unique in Alcoholics Anonymous. Unless each A.A. member follows to the best of his ability our suggested Twelve Steps to recovery, he almost certainly signs his own death warrant. His drunkenness and dissolution are not penalties inflicted by people in authority; they result from his personal disobedience to spiritual principles.

The same stern threat applies to the group itself. Unless there is approximate conformity to A.A.'s Twelve Traditions, the group, too, can deteriorate and die. So we of A.A. do obey spiritual principles, first because we must, and ultimately because we love the kind of life such obedience brings. Great suffering and great love are A.A.'s disciplinarians; we need no others.

It is clear now that we ought never to name boards to govern us, but it is equally clear that we shall always need to authorize workers to serve us. It is the difference between the spirit of vested authority and the spirit of service, two concepts which are sometimes poles apart. It is in this spirit of service that we elect the A.A. group's informal rotating committee, the intergroup association for the area, and the General Service Conferences of Alcoholics Anonymous for A.A. as a whole. Even our Foundation, once an independent board, is today directly accountable to our Fellowship. Its trustees are the caretakers and expediters of our world services.

Just as the aim of each A.A. member is personal sobriety, the aim of our services is to bring sobriety within reach of all who want it. If nobody does the group's chores, if the area's telephone rings unanswered, if we do not reply to our mail, then A.A. as we know it would stop. Our communications lines with those who need our help would be broken.

A.A. has to function, but at the same time it must avoid those dangers of great wealth, prestige, and entrenched power which necessarily tempt other societies. Though Tradition Nine at first sight seems to deal with a purely practical matter, in its actual operation it discloses a society without organization, animated only by the spirit of service—a true fellowship.

Tradition Ten

"Alcoholics Anonymous has no opinion on out-side issues; hence the A.A. name ought never be drawn into public controversy."

NEVER since it began has Alcoholics Anonymous been divided by a major controversial issue. Nor has our Fellowship ever publicly taken sides on any question in an embattled world. This, however, has been no earned virtue. It could almost be said that we were born with it, for, as one oldtimer recently declared, "Practically never have I heard a heated religious, political, or reform argument among A.A. members. So long as we don't argue these matters privately, it's a cinch we never shall publicly."

As by some deep instinct, we A.A.'s have known from the very beginning that we must never, no matter what the provocation, publicly take sides in any fight, even a worthy one. All history affords us the spectacle of striving nations and groups finally torn asunder because they were designed for, or tempted into, controversy. Others fell apart because of sheer self-righteousness while trying to enforce upon the rest of mankind some millennium of their own specification. In our own times, we have seen millions die in political and economic wars often spurred by religious and racial difference. We live in the imminent possibility of a fresh holocaust to determine how men shall be governed, and how the products of nature and toil shall be divided among them. That is the spiritual climate in which A.A. was born, and by God's grace has nevertheless flourished.

Let us reemphasize that this reluctance to fight one another or anybody else is not counted as some special virtue which makes us feel superior to other people. Nor does it mean that the members of Alcoholics Anonymous, now restored as citizens of the world, are going to back away from their individual responsibilities to act as they see the right upon issues of our time. But when it comes to A.A. as a whole, that's quite a different matter. In this respect, we do not enter into public controversy, because we know that our Society will perish if it does. We conceive the survival and spread of Alcoholics Anonymous to be something of far greater importance than the weight we could collectively throw back of any other cause. Since recovery from alcoholism is life itself to us, it is imperative that we preserve in full strength our means of survival.

Maybe this sounds as though the alcoholics in A.A. had suddenly gone peaceable, and become one great big happy family. Of course, this isn't so at all. Human beings that we are, we squabble. Before we leveled off a bit, A.A. looked more like one prodigious squabble than anything else, at least on the surface. A corporation director who had just voted a company expenditure of a hundred thousand dollars would appear at an A.A. business meeting and blow his top over an outlay of twenty-five dollars' worth of needed postage stamps. Disliking the attempt of some to manage a group, half its membership might angrily rush off to form another group more to their liking. Elders, temporarily turned Pharisee, have sulked. Bitter attacks have been directed against people suspected of mixed motives. Despite their din, our puny rows never did A.A. a particle of harm. They were just part and parcel of learning to work and live together. Let it be noted, too, that they were almost always concerned with ways to make A.A. more effective, how to do the most good for the most alcoholics.

The Washingtonian Society, a movement among alcoholics which started in Baltimore a century ago, almost discovered the answer to alcoholism. At first, the society was composed entirely of alcoholics trying to help one another. The early members foresaw that they should dedicate themselves to this sole aim. In many respects, the Washingtonians were akin to A.A. of today. Their membership passed the hundred thousand mark. Had they been left to themselves, and had they stuck to their one goal, they might have found the rest of the answer. But this didn't happen. Instead, the Washingtonians permitted politicians and reformers, both alcoholic and nonalcoholic, to use the society for their own purposes. Abolition of slavery, for example, was a stormy political issue then. Soon, Washingtonian speakers violently and publicly took sides on this question. Maybe the society could have survived the abolition controversy, but it didn't have a chance from the moment it determined to reform America's drinking habits. When the Washingtonians became temperance crusaders, within a very few years they had completely lost their effectiveness in helping alcoholics.

The lesson to be learned from the Washingtonians was not overlooked by Alcoholics Anonymous. As we surveyed the wreck of that movement, early A.A. members resolved to keep our Society out of public controversy. Thus was laid the cornerstone for Tradition Ten: "Alcoholics Anonymous has no opinion on outside issues; hence the A.A. name ought never be drawn into public controversy."

Tradition Eleven

"Our public relations policy is based on attraction rather than promotion; we need always maintain personal anonymity at the level of press, radio, and films."

WITHOUT its legions of well-wishers, A.A. could never have grown as it has. Throughout the world, immense and favorable publicity of every description has been the principal means of bringing alcoholics into our Fellowship. In A.A. offices, clubs, and homes, telephones ring constantly. One voice says, "I read a piece in the newspapers..."; another, "We heard a radio program..."; and still another, "We saw a moving picture..." or "We saw something about A.A. on television...." It is no exaggeration to say that half of A.A.'s membership has been led to us through channels like these.

The inquiring voices are not all alcoholics or their families. Doctors read medical papers about Alcoholics Anonymous and call for more information. Clergymen see articles in their church journals and also make inquiries. Employers learn that great corporations have set their approval upon us, and wish to discover what can be done about alcoholism in their own firms.

Therefore, a great responsibility fell upon us to develop the best possible public relations policy for Alcoholics Anonymous. Through many painful experiences, we think we have arrived at what that policy ought to be. It is the opposite in many ways of usual promotional practice. We found that we had to rely upon the principle of *attraction* rather than of promotion.

Let's see how these two contrasting ideas—attraction and promotion—work out. A political party wishes to win an election, so it advertises the virtues of its leadership to draw votes. A worthy charity wants to raise money; forthwith, its letterhead shows the name of every distinguished person whose support can be obtained. Much of the political, economic, and religious life of the world is dependent upon publicized leadership. People who symbolize causes and ideas fill a deep human need. We of A.A. do not question that. But we do have to soberly face the fact that being in the public eye is hazardous, especially for us. By temperament, nearly every one of us had been an irrepressible promoter, and the prospect of a society composed almost entirely of promoters was frightening. Considering this explosive factor, we knew we had to exercise self-restraint.

The way this restraint paid off was startling. It resulted in more favorable publicity of Alcoholics Anonymous than could possibly have been obtained through all the arts and abilities of A.A.'s best press agents. Obviously, A.A. had to be publicized somehow, so we resorted to the idea that it would be far better to let our friends do this for us. Precisely that has happened, to an unbelievable extent. Veteran newsmen, trained doubters that they are, have gone all out to carry A.A.'s message. To them, we are something more than the source of good stories. On almost every newsfront, the men and women of the press have attached themselves to us as friends.

In the beginning, the press could not understand our re-
fusal of all personal publicity. They were genuinely baffled
by our insistence upon anonymity. Then they got the point.
Here was something rare in the world—a society which
said it wished to publicize its principles and its work, but
not its individual members. The press was delighted with
this attitude. Ever since, these friends have reported A.A.
with an enthusiasm which the most ardent members would
find hard to match.

There was actually a time when the press of America
thought the anonymity of A.A. was better for us than
some of our own members did. At one point, about a hundred of our Society were breaking anonymity at the public level. With perfectly good intent, these folks declared
that the principle of anonymity was horse-and-buggy
stuff, something appropriate to A.A.'s pioneering days.
They were sure that A.A. could go faster and farther if
it availed itself of modern publicity methods. A.A., they
pointed out, included many persons of local, national,
or international fame. Provided they were willing—and
many were—why shouldn't their membership be publicized, thereby encouraging others to join us? These were
plausible arguments, but happily our friends of the writing profession disagreed with them.

The Foundation* wrote letters to practically every news
outlet in North America, setting forth our public relations

---

* In 1954, the name of the Alcoholic Foundation, Inc., was changed to the General
Service Board of Alcoholics Anonymous, Inc., and the Foundation office is now
the General Service Office.

policy of attraction rather than promotion, and emphasizing personal anonymity as A.A.'s greatest protection. Since that time, editors and rewrite men have repeatedly deleted names and pictures of members from A.A. copy; frequently, they have reminded ambitious individuals of A.A.'s anonymity policy. They have even sacrificed good stories to this end. The force of their cooperation has certainly helped. Only a few A.A. members are left who deliberately break anonymity at the public level.

This, in brief, is the process by which A.A.'s Tradition Eleven was constructed. To us, however, it represents far more than a sound public relations policy. It is more than a denial of self-seeking. This Tradition is a constant and practical reminder that personal ambition has no place in A.A. In it, each member becomes an active guardian of our Fellowship.

Tradition Twelve

"Anonymity is the spiritual foundation of all our traditions, ever reminding us to place principles before personalities."

THE spiritual substance of anonymity is sacrifice. Because A.A.'s Twelve Traditions repeatedly ask us to give up personal desires for the common good, we realize that the sacrificial spirit—well symbolized by anonymity—is the foundation of them all. It is A.A.'s proved willingness to make these sacrifices that gives people their high confidence in our future.

But in the beginning, anonymity was not born of confidence; it was the child of our early fears. Our first nameless groups of alcoholics were secret societies. New prospects could find us only through a few trusted friends. The bare hint of publicity, even for our work, shocked us. Though ex-drinkers, we still thought we had to hide from public distrust and contempt.

When the Big Book appeared in 1939, we called it "Alcoholics Anonymous." Its foreword made this revealing statement: "It is important that we remain anonymous because we are too few, at present, to handle the overwhelming number of personal appeals which may result from this publication. Being mostly business or professional folk, we could not well carry on our occupations in such an event." Between these lines, it is easy to read our fear that large numbers of incoming people might break our anonymity wide open.

As the A.A. groups multiplied, so did anonymity problems. Enthusiastic over the spectacular recovery of a brother alcoholic, we'd sometimes discuss those intimate and harrowing aspects of his case meant for his sponsor's ear alone. The aggrieved victim would then rightly declare that his trust had been broken. When such stories got into circulation outside of A.A., the loss of confidence in our anonymity promise was severe. It frequently turned people from us. Clearly, every A.A. member's name—and story, too—had to be confidential, if he wished. This was our first lesson in the practical application of anonymity.

With characteristic intemperance, however, some of our newcomers cared not at all for secrecy. They wanted to shout A.A. from the housetops, and did. Alcoholics barely dry rushed about bright-eyed, buttonholing anyone who would listen to their stories. Others hurried to place themselves before microphones and cameras. Sometimes, they got distressingly drunk and let their groups down with a bang. They had changed from A.A. members into A.A. show-offs.

This phenomenon of contrast really set us thinking. Squarely before us was the question "How anonymous should an A.A. member be?" Our growth made it plain that we couldn't be a secret society, but it was equally plain that we couldn't be a vaudeville circuit, either. The charting of a safe path between these extremes took a long time.

As a rule, the average newcomer wanted his family to know immediately what he was trying to do. He also wanted to tell others who had tried to help him—his doctor, his minister, and close friends. As he gained confidence, he felt it right to explain his new way of life to his employer and business associates. When opportunities to be helpful came along, he found he could talk easily about A.A. to almost anyone. These quiet disclosures helped him to lose his fear of the alcoholic stigma, and spread the news of A.A.'s existence in his community. Many a new man and woman came to A.A. because of such conversations. Though not in the strict letter of anonymity, such communications were well within its spirit.

But it became apparent that the word-of-mouth method was too limited. Our work, as such, needed to be publicized. The A.A. groups would have to reach quickly as many despairing alcoholics as they could. Consequently, many groups began to hold meetings which were open to interested friends and the public, so that the average citizen could see for himself just what A.A. was all about. The response to these meetings was warmly sympathetic. Soon, groups began to receive requests for A.A. speakers to appear before civic organizations, church groups, and medical societies. Provided anonymity was maintained on these platforms, and reporters present were cautioned against the use of names or pictures, the result was fine.

Then came our first few excursions into major publicity, which were breathtaking. Cleveland's *Plain Dealer* articles about us ran that town's membership from a few into hundreds overnight. The news stories of Mr. Rockefeller's dinner for Alcoholics Anonymous helped double our total membership in a year's time. Jack Alexander's famous

Saturday Evening Post piece made A.A. a national institution. Such tributes as these brought opportunities for still more recognition. Other newspapers and magazines wanted A.A. stories. Film companies wanted to photograph us. Radio, and finally television, besieged us with requests for appearances. What should we do?

As this tide offering top public approval swept in, we realized that it could do us incalculable good or great harm. Everything would depend upon how it was channeled. We simply couldn't afford to take the chance of letting self-appointed members present themselves as messiahs representing A.A. before the whole public. The promoter instinct in us might be our undoing. If even one publicly got drunk, or was lured into using A.A.'s name for his own purposes, the damage might be irreparable. At this altitude (press, radio, films, and television), anonymity—100 percent anonymity—was the only possible answer. Here, principles would have to come before personalities, without exception.

These experiences taught us that anonymity is real humility at work. It is an all-pervading spiritual quality which today keynotes A.A. life everywhere. Moved by the spirit of anonymity, we try to give up our natural desires for personal distinction as A.A. members both among fellow alcoholics and before the general public. As we lay aside these very human aspirations, we believe that each of us takes part in the weaving of a protective mantle which covers our whole Society and under which we may grow and work in unity.

We are sure that humility, expressed by anonymity, is the greatest safeguard that Alcoholics Anonymous can ever have.

The Twelve Traditions
(The Long Form)

Our A.A. experience has taught us that:

One—Each member of Alcoholics Anonymous is but a small part of a great whole. A.A. must continue to live or most of us will surely die. Hence our common welfare comes first. But individual welfare follows close afterward.

Two—For our group purpose there is but one ultimate authority—a loving God as He may express Himself in our group conscience.

Three—Our membership ought to include all who suffer from alcoholism. Hence we may refuse none who wish to recover. Nor ought A.A. membership ever depend upon money or conformity. Any two or three alcoholics gathered together for sobriety may call themselves an A.A. group, provided that, as a group, they have no other affiliation.

Four—With respect to its own affairs, each A.A. group should be responsible to no other authority than its own conscience. But when its plans concern the welfare of neighboring groups also, those groups ought to be consulted. And no group, regional committee, or individual should ever take any action that might greatly affect A.A. as a whole without conferring with the trustees of the General Service Board. On such issues our common welfare is paramount.

Five—Each Alcoholics Anonymous group ought to be a spiritual entity *having but one primary purpose*—that of carrying its message to the alcoholic who still suffers.

Six—Problems of money, property, and authority may easily divert us from our primary spiritual aim. We think, therefore, that any considerable property of genuine use to A.A. should be separately incorporated and managed, thus dividing the material from the spiritual. An A.A. group, as such, should never go into business. Secondary aids to A.A., such as clubs or hospitals which require much property or administration, ought to be incorporated and so set apart that, if necessary, they can be freely discarded by the groups. Hence such facilities ought not to use the A.A. name. Their management should be the sole responsibility of those people who financially support them. For clubs, A.A. managers are usually preferred. But hospitals, as well as other places of recuperation, ought to be well outside A.A.—and medically supervised. While an A.A. group may cooperate with anyone, such cooperation ought never to go so far as affiliation or endorsement, actual or implied. An A.A. group can bind itself to no one.

Seven—The A.A. groups themselves ought to be fully supported by the voluntary contributions of their own members. We think that each group should soon achieve this ideal; that any public solicitation of funds using the name of Alcoholics Anonymous is highly dangerous, whether by groups, clubs, hospitals, or other outside agencies; that acceptance of large gifts from any source, or of contributions carrying any obligation whatever, is unwise. Then, too, we view with much concern those A.A. treasuries which continue, beyond prudent reserves, to accumulate funds for no stated A.A. purpose. Experience has often warned us that nothing can so surely destroy our spiritual heritage as futile disputes over property, money, and authority.

Eight—Alcoholics Anonymous should remain forever nonprofessional. We define professionalism as the occupation of counseling alcoholics for fees or hire. But we may employ alcoholics where they are going to perform those services for which we might otherwise have to engage nonalcoholics. Such special services may be well recompensed. But our usual A.A. Twelfth Step work is never to be paid for.

Nine—Each A.A. group needs the least possible organization. Rotating leadership is the best. The small group may elect its secretary, the large group its rotating committee, and the groups of a large metropolitan area their central or intergroup committee, which often employs a full-time secretary. The trustees of the General Service Board are, in effect, our A.A. General Service Committee. They are the custodians of our A.A. Tradition and the receivers of voluntary A.A. contributions by which we maintain our A.A. General Service Office at New York. They are authorized by the groups to handle our overall public relations and they guarantee the integrity of our principal newspaper, the A.A. Grapevine. All such representatives are to be guided in the spirit of service, for true leaders in A.A. are but trusted and experienced servants of the whole. They derive no real authority from their titles; they do not govern. Universal respect is the key to their usefulness.

Ten—No A.A. group or member should ever, in such a way as to implicate A.A., express any opinion on outside controversial issues—particularly those of politics, alcohol reform, or sectarian religion. The Alcoholics Anonymous groups oppose no one. Concerning such matters they can express no views whatever.

Eleven—Our relations with the general public should be characterized by personal anonymity. We think A.A. ought to avoid sensational advertising. Our names and pictures as A.A. members ought not be broadcast, filmed, or publicly printed. Our public relations should be guided by the principle of attraction rather than promotion. There is never need to praise ourselves. We feel it better to let our friends recommend us.

Twelve—And finally, we of Alcoholics Anonymous believe that the principle of anonymity has an immense spiritual significance. It reminds us that we are to place principles before personalities; that we are actually to practice a genuine humility. This to the end that our great blessings may never spoil us; that we shall forever live in thankful contemplation of Him who presides over us all.

ISBN-13: 978-0-916856-06-9

9 780916 856069